Trust and Economics

A great deal of attention has been given recently to one of the central paradoxes of trust: namely how people can restrict self-interest in order to trust. Existing perspectives, theories, and models offer partial explanations, but this volume presents a novel framework that expands on the findings of recent studies of trust and exchange. This book offers a new angle for the understanding of exchange and trust in an interactive context, describes the interactive characteristics of trust in exchange systems, and develops a theory explaining the co-evolution of trust and exchange systems.

A new framework is used to incorporate the theory of systems of trust and evolutionary game-theoretical approach to investigate four important questions: How can trust emerge in exchange when people pursue self-interest? After its emergence, how does exchange affect trust in a dynamic process? When are dynamics of trust stable? Do interactive trust phenomena differ under different exchange systems? This book concludes with a discussion of the implications of the theoretical findings for three areas: the improvement of trust, potential economic growth, and mechanism design in exchange systems.

This volume makes a significant contribution to the literature on evolutionary and institutional economics and is suitable for those who have an interest in political economy, economy theory and philosophy as well as economic psychology.

Yanlong Zhang is a Research Assistant at the Institute of Economics at Isinghua University, China.

Routledge Advances in Heterodox Economics
Edited by Wolfram Elsner of University of Bremen and
Peter Kriesler of University of New South Wales

Over the past two decades, the intellectual agendas of heterodox economists have taken a decidedly pluralist turn. Leading thinkers have begun to move beyond the established paradigms of Austrian, feminist, Institutional-evolutionary, Marxian, post Keynesian, radical, social, and Sraffian economics – opening up new lines of analysis, criticism, and dialogue among dissenting schools of thought. This cross-fertilization of ideas is creating a new generation of scholarship in which novel combinations of heterodox ideas are being brought to bear on important contemporary and historical problems.

Routledge Advances in Heterodox Economics aims to promote this new scholarship by publishing innovative books in heterodox economic theory, policy, philosophy, intellectual history, institutional history, and pedagogy. Syntheses or critical engagement of two or more heterodox traditions are especially encouraged.

21. An Ecosystem Approach to Economic Stabilization
Escaping the neoliberal wilderness
Rodrick Wallace

22. The Economic Crisis in Social and Institutional Context
Theories, policies and exit strategies

Edited by Pasquale Tridico and Sebastiano Fadda

23. Trust and Economics
The co-evolution of trust and exchange systems
Yanlong Zhang

This series was previously published by The University of Michigan Press and the following books are available (please contact UMP for more information):

Economics in Real Time
A Theoretical Reconstruction
John McDermott

Liberating Economics
Feminist Perspectives on Families, Work, and Globalization
Drucilla K. Barker and Susan F. Feiner

Socialism After Hayek
Theodore A. Burczak

Future Directions for Heterodox Economics
Edited by John T. Harvey and Robert F. Garnett, Jr.

Are Worker Rights Human Rights?
Richard P. McIntyre

Trust and Economics

The co-evolution of trust and exchange systems

Yanlong Zhang

Routledge
Taylor & Francis Group

LONDON AND NEW YORK

First published 2016 by Routledge

2 Park Square, Milton Park, Abingdon, Oxfordshire OX14 4RN
52 Vanderbilt Avenue, New York, NY 10017

Routledge is an imprint of the Taylor & Francis Group, an informa business

First issued in paperback 2020

British Library Cataloguing in Publication Data
A catalogue record for this book is available from the British Library

Library of Congress Cataloging in Publication Data
Zhang, Yanlong, 1980–
Trust and economics: the co-evolution of trust and exchange systems/
Yanlong Zhang.
pages cm
1. Trust—Economic aspects. 2. Exchange. 3. Economics. I. Title.
HB72.Z4366 2015
306.3′4–dc23
2015002310

ISBN: 978-1-138-86095-7 (hbk)
ISBN: 978-0-367-59883-9 (pbk)

Typeset in Times New Roman
by Swales & Willis Ltd, Exeter, Devon, UK

To my father

Contents

Figures

Tables

Preface

This book is composed of my doctoral dissertation, which was used to complete my PhD degree at the University of Bremen, Germany. The book offers a new angle for understanding exchange and trust in an interactive context, describes the interactive characteristics of trust in exchange systems, and develops a theory of the co-evolution of trust and exchange systems.

Acknowledgments

I record my special thanks to Professor Wolfram Elsner for his supervision and active support for the book and to the China Scholarship Council for granting me a scholarship. I am also grateful to Andy Humphries, senior editor in Economics at Routledge, as well as Peter Kriesler and Mark Setterfield, series editors of Routledge Advances in Heterodox Economics. I also obtained comments from my colleagues at Bremen and language services from Editage. Furthermore, I thank the following for all their discussions and advice: Shuanping Dai, University of Duisburg-Essen; Tong-Yaa Su and Xingting Liu, both University of Bremen; Yuanheng Li, University of Goettingen; Fei Ai, Chinese Academy of Science; Xiaolei Liu, MIT; and Wenhao Song, University of Shanghai Jiao Tong.

Abbreviations

B2B   Business to Business
C2C   Consumer to Consumer
EGT   Evolutionary Game Theory
ESS   Evolutionarily Stable Strategy
GDP   Gross Domestic Product
PD   Prisoner's Dilemma
RCT   Rational Choice Theory
SS   Stable State
TCT   Transaction Cost Theory

1   Introduction

In economics, exchange (e.g., Walrasian exchange) is often identified as a static thing through which assorted equilibria are technically feasible in a whole economy. The phenomena and problems inherent in this dynamic process, however, have not thus far been studied extensively, with the exception of the few economists that have examined the importance of the trust–exchange relationship (Williamson, 1993; Perelman, 1998). Based on this gap in the body of knowledge, this study presents trust and exchange systems in a unified framework (evolutionary economics) and then offers improvements and extensions.

Although exchange and trust have co-evolved historically, these twin concepts have been largely overlooked by economic studies, which have generally treated exchange (i) as a static process rather than an interactive dynamic one and (ii) as trust being implicitly rather than explicitly presupposed (i.e., barter, monetary, and Internet trust exchanges all belong to the same entity – exchange). If we consider the economics of trust to be a social action (Coleman, 1982) under uncertainty, then "there is an element of trust in every transaction" (Arrow, 1973, p. 24). Moreover, trust is placed in "transitions between micro-level individual actions and macro-level states of the system" (Möllering, 2006, p. 15), suggesting trust phenomena (i.e., emergence, evolution, and stability) exist in interactive processes in exchange systems (Elsner and Schwardt, 2014), as this book further explores. More specifically, the motivation for this study is to describe the interactive dynamic characteristics of trust in exchange systems in general and to draw conclusions on the co-evolution of trust and exchange systems in particular in order to enrich recent studies in this body of research.

The importance of trust in exchange

The importance of trust in exchange has been emphasized in a number of economic studies (Table 1.1 lists the important works in this regard). The literature suggests that trust is the foundation of exchange in various ways. First, trust is related to transaction costs (e.g., Williamson, 1985; North, 1990). The emergence of trust helps reduce transaction costs among and between firms, collectives, and individuals, which serves as "an important lubricant of a social system" (Arrow, 1974, p. 23). Second, trust is intrinsically related to the principal's problem (e.g., Ross, 1973; Shapiro, 1987) of not trusting his or her agents to handle certain issues capably. Third, trust is utilized to form an exchange relationship (e.g., Gulati, 1995; Das and Teng, 2001; Poppo and Zenger, 2002) that reinforces the cooperation between the parties. Finally, trust is described as taking part in expectation theory in the exchange (e.g., Simmel, 1990; Möllering, 2001; Elsner and Schwardt, 2014), which suggests that expectation is a source of trust. In summary, "there is an element of trust in every transaction" (Arrow, 1973, p. 24).

Indeed, the importance of trust is not limited to the domain of economics. Management (e.g., Macaulay, 1963; Emerson, 1978; La Porta *et al.*, 1997; Bigley and Pearce, 1998; Levi, 1998), sociology (e.g., Blau, 1964; Deutsch,

Table 1.1 Themes and sources of trust in economic exchange

Themes	Sources
Trust and transaction cost theory (TCT)	North (1990), Williamson (1985), Cummings and Bromiley (1996), Bigley and Pearce (1998)
Trust and agency theory	Ross (1973), Shapiro (1987), Eisenhardt (1989), Möllering (2006)
Trust and exchange relationship	Granovetter (1985), Das and Teng (2001), Gulati (1995), Dyer (2000), Poppo and Zenger (2002)
Trust and expectation	Fox (1974), Luhman (1979), Lewis and Weigert (1985), Coleman (1990), Misztal (1996) Möllering (2006), Gambetta (1988), Simmel (1990), Elsner and Schwardt (2014)
Trust and exchange structure	Akerlof (1970), Siamwalla (1978), Popkin (1981), Kollock (1994)
Trust, reputation and reciprocity	Trivers (1971), Greif (1989), Lahno (1995), Hardin (2000), Milinski *et al.* (2002), Resnick and Zeckhauser (2002), Nowak and Sigmund (1998)
Trust and exchange arena size	Friedman (1979), Landa (1981, 1994), Berman (1983), Milgrom *et al.* (1990), Bernstein (1996), Stringham (2002), Leeson (2008), Elsner and Heinrich (2009), Elsner and Schwardt (2014)

1973; Dawes, 1980; Cook and Hardin, 2001; Nickel and Vaesen, 2012), and biology (e.g., Hirshleifer, 2001), from different perspectives, relatively or distinctly, explain its function and promote its development in the academic world. This interdisciplinary consensus on the importance of trust raises the question of what makes it so important. As a partial explanation, before elaborating on this answer explicitly herein, the paradoxes inherent in trust-building provoke deep and relevant questions.

The paradoxes of trust

In previous studies (see Table 1.1), trust is generally defined as a rational choice in the exchange process, together with decisions on whether trust ought to be placed at risk. According to Gambetta (1988), "When we say we trust someone or that someone is trustworthy, we implicitly mean that the probability that he will perform an action that is beneficial or at least not detrimental to us is high enough for us to consider engaging in some form of cooperation with him" (p. 217). Further, as Coleman (1990) argued, trust is a rational choice in "situations in which the risk one takes depends on the performance of another actor" (p. 91; see also Hosmer, 1995; Lane, 1998; Whitener *et al.*, 1998).

Despite the existence of rationality in this regard, people are constrained by different incentive structures in exchange such as in prisoner's dilemma (PD) games. Furthermore, uncertainties in the exchange relationship also influence the extent to which parties can be trusted. One paradox of trust is thus the degree to which people can restrict their own self-interest (James, 2002). Put differently, what makes one person place trust in another when irregular behavior is likely to occur in a certain incentive structure?

Another paradox is that if trust is critical for exchange, why cannot trust simply be presumed (in other words, exchange is also important for trust)? There may be two reasons for this. On the one hand, trust may be an outcome of a dynamic exchange. For example, as Simmel (1990) stated, interactions form the starting point of all phenomena in society and, of these, exchange is a basic and important interactive process that influences trust-building. On the other hand, trust seems to be a result of static exchange (i.e., unrepeated exchange), because exchange itself may provide the "incentive" to trust. For example, if a person wants to buy a secondhand car, he or she should find out about any pre-existing mechanical problems. Alternatively, in international trade, as many studies have shown, although payment to a company abroad is typically made in advance, the goods cannot be exchanged simultaneously. This divergence may cause a lack of trust because finding faults with goods takes a long time, within which period cheaters may have already fled.

Existing explanations

Although people experience matters relevant to trust every day, it is still difficult to grasp the paradoxes of trust at the abstract level. The questions of how people can restrict self-interest in a certain incentive structure in order to trust and how exchange affects trust in either static or dynamic contexts are dependent on distinct perspectives and different theoretical approaches. One of the most common theories in this respect is rational choice theory (RCT). The rationality-based view (e.g., Deutsch, 1973; Coleman, 1982; Frank, 1987; Hollis, 1998; Dasgupta, 2000; James, 2002; Möllering, 2006) has demonstrated that trust is often riskily placed in interactions because of the existing incentives to assess the underlying losses and rewards rationally. As Gambetta (1988) defined, trust is considered to exist when "the probability that the trustee will perform an action that is beneficial or at least not detrimental to us is high enough for us to consider engaging in some form of cooperation with him" (p. 217). Or as Möllering (2001) argued, trust is "a state of favorable expectation regarding other individual actions and intentions" (p. 404). Although there exist conflicts in incentives for trust in these studies (i.e., expectation, reason, and calculation), trust is confined to rational models, which is an important step for perceiving one of the paradoxes of trust, namely how people can restrict self-interest in order to trust.

This perspective on exchange in the second paradox of trust stems from game-theoretical models, which are often used to describe exchange in everyday life (e.g., Deutsch, 1960; Hardin, 2006). Specifically, the emergence of better-off equilibria in models means the emergence of trust in particular, while worse-off equilibria often lead to distrust in general because of the conflicts inherent in exchange. In particular, from this perspective, trust is considered to be a static interaction of exchange or to exist in local interactions (e.g., studies of trust experiments), and is less related to dynamic or global interaction. This gap is bridged in this study because of the large interactive process of exchange in which trust phenomena develop.

Another important and oft-cited theory is the institution-based view (e.g., Schotter, 1981; Zucker, 1986; Knight, 1990; Powell and DiMaggio, 1991; Levi, 1998), which explains the paradoxes of trust based on two points: *trust in institutions* and *institutional change*. The first point refers to the fact that placing trust in a stable environment is *isomorphized* by institutions in which everyone carries out predictable and routinized actions. In other words, "trust has to be achieved with a *familiar* world" (Luhmann, 1988, p. 95). Then, because institutional change reduces or increases reliable functioning, this degree of *familiarity* affects the dynamics of trust. Put another way, the dynamics of trust comply with institutional change. Hence, it serves to be an implication that the evolution of exchange systems describes different dynamic trust phenomena.

The third theoretical vantage point is the empiricism-based view (e.g., Miller, 1974; Knack and Keefer, 1997; La Porta *et al.*, 1997; Stolle, 1998; Yamagishi *et al.*, 1998; Knack and Zak, 2002; Uslaner, 2002; Dincer and Uslaner, 2010). Through theoretical models and hypothesis building, this perspective has shown that the paradoxes of trust are achieved by empirical outcomes in which the determinants of trust are found. These independent factors belong to extensive categories (e.g., life satisfaction, institutional efficiency, group size) in the broader sense, depending on those that place trust. Further, despite the importance of understanding causes for the emergence of trust, the dynamic process between independent and dependent issues is lacking, which prevents us from understanding how trust is influenced in dynamic exchange as well as from finding out interactive phenomena in a direct way.

Among these views on the paradoxes of trust, consensus exists that explanations are limited to the static context, failing to acknowledge the presence of an interactive process and overlooking the differences in interactive trust phenomena in exchange systems. Indeed, views on the issues examined in this study include the process-based view (e.g., Lave and March, 1975; Eisenhardt, 1989), the society-based view (e.g., Fukuyama, 1995; Sztompka, 1999), and the transaction cost-based view (e.g., Williamson, 1975). While these perspectives, theories, and models offer partial explanations of one of the paradoxes of trust, this study combines all the paradoxes of trust and describes interactive trust phenomena in a novel framework that expands on the findings of recent studies of trust and exchange.

Research questions and framework

Based on the above, the present study aims to answer the following four research questions:

1 How can trust emerge in exchange?
2 After its emergence, how does exchange affect trust in the dynamic process (i.e., how does trust evolve)?
3 When are the dynamics of trust stable?
4 Do interactive trust phenomena differ under different exchange systems (e.g., barter, monetary, Internet)?

To help answer these questions, I first introduce the framework that is expected to contribute to the body of research on trust in evolutionary economics.

This framework begins with the theory of the system of trust provided by Coleman (1990). This theory is developed partly based on the basic literature on evolutionary economics, such as Maynard Smith (1982) and Maynard Smith and Price (1973). Moreover, Coleman's theory constrains a set of economic agents, a set of actions, and a set of rules as subsystems in exchange. Thus, it offers the foundation for studying how interactive exchange organizes the trust in complex settings in order to describe interactive trust phenomena (i.e., evolution and stability). As the theory of trust implies, different exchange systems (i.e., barter, monetary, Internet) are considered through an analysis of interactive structures, which serves to argue that different exchange systems present interactive trust phenomena because of the emergence of interactive structures.

Given the emergence of interactive structures in which agents act interdependently, the description of interactive trust phenomena requires an approach that is applicable in an interactive context. To be relevant, although the applicable context varies considerably, many studies have focused on the evolutionary approach in order to classify interactive processes in the system of trust under interactive exchange structures into three types of analysis, namely the emergence, evolution, and stability of trust (for more details, see Chapter 3).

As mentioned, the main characteristic of this framework is that it views trust in exchange as a *system of trust* (see Figure 2.4) that comprises the following three components: "Purposive actions of individual actors, deciding to place or withdraw trust or to break or keep trust; the micro-to-macro transition . . . ; and the macro-to-micro transition . . ." (Coleman, 1990, p. 175). Within these three components, emergence, evolution, and stability are found in the evolutionary approach. Considering exchange and trust from this perspective has also been important for recent exchange studies, because this standpoint argues that exchange itself tends to be important for trust in an interactive context. This finding helps explain one of the paradoxes of trust and suggests a theory of the co-evolution of exchange systems and trust.

Outline of the study

This study is structured into seven chapters. Chapter 2 pays attention to the foundation of the theory of the co-evolution of exchange systems and trust in view of the findings on trust in recent economic studies, which suggest the theory of the system of trust as a proper theoretical foundation for this study. One of the important points that guide the co-evolution of exchange systems and trust is that the emergence of interactive structures influences interactive phenomena in the system of trust (e.g., the evolution and stability of trust). Therefore, these interactive structures are first identified and then summarized theoretically in this chapter.

Chapter 3 describes an evolutionary approach that analyzes, models, and displays the components of trust in this study. In particular, this chapter provides a detailed introduction of the structure of the approach, including its basic concepts and modeling process, which permeates the analysis in this study. It also provides a plan for the subsequent analysis and emphasizes that the evolutionary approach complements the analysis of the theory of the system of trust.

In Chapter 4, contingent on the theory and approach mentioned above, two main treatments are jointly considered, namely behavioral and evolutionary interdependences, in order to explain how trust emerges and to solve the paradox of trust. The former is limited to the emergence of trust in the context in which people act interdependently, but not in repeated exchanges (i.e., one-shot situations). The main theoretical concepts of expectation, reason, and calculation are extended to describe the emergence of trust under such circumstances. In evolutionary interdependence, the concept of imitating trust is provided in order to model emergence in dynamic (i.e., repeated) exchanges. Overall, this chapter aims to explain one of the paradoxes of trust identified in this study, namely how people can restrict self-interest in order to trust.

After describing the emergence of trust, Chapter 5 further explains how it evolves and stabilizes in exchange. For the evolution of trust, according to the theoretical approach presented in Chapter 3, the theoretical assumption about the co-evolution of exchange systems and trust is analyzed in three exchange scenarios, namely barter, monetary, and Internet. The results confirm our expectation that distinct interactive trust phenomena seem to be dependent on the interactive structures of exchange systems. This finding concurs with those of previous research, which has found that the stability of trust is susceptible to interactive structures and shows distinct features. This chapter thus complements the basic theory of the co-evolution of exchange systems and trust and provides a new orientation for trust and exchange studies.

Chapter 6 starts by emphasizing that the evolution of phenomena is affected by noises in the dynamic process (Foster and Young, 1990), suggesting that varieties of trust exist under combinations of influencing factors. Following this point, the evolution of trust is reconsidered once again in an overlapping network because empirical evidence shows the existence of an overlapping random effect between an interaction network and learning network, which creates a time lag to interact and results in turbulence. This chapter thus considers turbulences within the evolution process of trust as a cause for the varieties of trust in real interactions.

Finally, in Chapter 7 this study draws conclusions based on the theoretical results presented in previous chapters. These conclusions are organized into four aspects. First, core contributions include the main theoretical findings of this study together with the answers to each of the four research questions.

Second, methodological implications are elaborated on, including the findings of this study and extensions of this approach to future research on trust and exchange. Third, according to the theoretical findings, implications are offered in three areas: improvement of trust, potential economic growth, and mechanism design in exchange systems. Finally, suggestions for future studies are provided by analyzing the remaining gaps.

References

Akerlof, G.A. 1970. The Market for "Lemons": Quality Uncertainty and the Market Mechanism. *Quarterly Journal of Economics*, 84(3), 488–500.

Arrow, K.J. 1973. *Information and Economic Behavior*. Stockholm: Federation of Swedish Industries.

Arrow, K. 1974. *The Limits of Organization*. New York, NY: Basic Books.

Berman, H.J. 1983. *Law and Revolution*. Cambridge, MA: Harvard University Press.

Bernstein, L. 1996. Merchant Law in a Merchant Court: Rethinking the Code's Search for Immanent Business Norms. *University of Pennsylvania Law Review*, 144, 1765–1821.

Bigley, G.A., Pearce, J.L. 1998. Straining for Shared Meaning in Organization Science: Problems of Trust and Distrust. *Academy of Management Review*, 23(3), 405–421.

Blau, P. 1964. *Exchange and Power in Social Life*. London: John Wiley.

Coleman, J.S. 1982. Systems of Trust: A Rough Theoretical Framework. *Angewandte Sozial-forschung*, 10(3), 277–299.

Coleman, J.S. 1990. *Foundations of Social Theory*. Cambridge, MA: Harvard University Press.

Cook, K.S., Hardin, R. 2001. Norms of Cooperativeness and Networks of Trust. In: Hech-ter, M., Opp, K. D. (Eds), *Social Norms*. New York, NY: Russell Sage, 327–347.

Cummings, L.L., Bromiley, P. 1996. The Organizational Trust Inventory (OTI): Development and Validation. In: Kramer, R.M., Tyler, T.R. (Eds), *Trust in Organizations*. Thousand Oaks, CA: Sage, 302–330.

Das, T.K., Teng, B.S. 2001. Trust, Control, and Risk in Strategic Alliances: An Integrated Framework. *Organization Studies*, 22, 251–283.

Dasgupta, P. 2000. Trust as a Commodity. In: Gambetta, D. (Ed.), *Trust: Making and Breaking Cooperative Relation*. Oxford: University of Oxford, 49–72.

Dawes, R.M. 1980. Social Dilemmas. *Annual Review of Psychology*, 31, 169–193.

Deutsch, M. 1960. Trust, Trustworthiness, and F-scale. *Journal of Abnormal and Social Psychology*, 61, 138–140.

Deutsch, M. 1973. *The Resolution of Conflict*. New Haven, CT: Yale University Press.

Dincer, O., Uslaner, E. 2010. Trust and Growth. *Public Choice*, 142, 58–67.

Dyer, J. 2000. The Determinants of Trust in Supplier–Buyer Relations in the U.S., Japan, and Korea. *Journal of International Business Studies*, 31, 259–285.

Eisenhardt, K.M. 1989. Agency Theory: An Assessment and Review. *Academy of Management Review*, 14(1), 57–74.

Elsner, W., Heinrich, T. 2009. A Simple Theory of "Meso": On the Co-evolution of Institutions and Platform Size – With an Application to Varieties of Capitalism and "Mediumsized" Countries. *Journal of Socio-Economics*, 38(5), 843–858.

Elsner, W., Schwardt, H. 2014. Trust and Arena Size: Expectations, Institutions, and General Trust, and Critical Population and Group Sizes. *Journal of Institutional Economics*, 10(1), 107–134.

Emerson, R.M. 1978. Power, Equity and Commitment in Exchange Networks. *American Sociological Review*, 43, 721–739.

Foster, D., Young, P. 1990. Stochastic Evolutionary Game Dynamics. *Theoretical Population Biology*, 38(2), 219–232.

Fox, A. 1974. *Beyond Contract: Work, Power and Trust Relations*. London: Faber and Faber.

Frank, R.H. 1987. If Homo Economicus Could Choose His Own Utility Function, Would He Want One with a Conscience? *American Economic Review*, 77(4), 593–604.

Friedman, D. 1979. Private Creation and Enforcement of Law: A Historical Case. *Journal of Legal Studies*, 8, 399–415.

Fukuyama, F. 1995. *Trust: Social Virtues and Creation of Prosperity*. New York, NY: Free Press.

Gambetta, D. 1988. Can We Trust in Trust? In: Gambetta, D. (Ed.), *Trust: Making and Breaking Cooperative Relations*. New York, NY: University of Oxford, 213–237.

Granovetter, M.S. 1985. Economic Action and Social Structure: The Problem of Embeddedness. *American Journal of Sociology*, 91, 481–510.

Greif, A. 1989. Reputation and Coalitions in Medieval Trade: Evidence on the Maghribi Traders. *Journal of Economic History*, 49(4), 857–881.

Gulati, R. 1995. Does Familiarity Breed Trust? The Implications of Repeated Ties for Contractual Choice in Alliances. *Academy of Management Journal*, 38, 85–112.

Hardin, R. 2000. *Trust and Society*. In: Galeotti, G., Salmon, P., Wintrobe, R. (Eds), *Competition and Structure: The Political Economy of Collective Decisions*. Cambridge, UK: Cambridge University Press, 23–43.

Hardin, R. 2006. *Trust: Key Concepts*. Cambridge, UK: Polity Press.

Hirshleifer, J. 2001. Game-Theoretic Interpretations of Commitment. In: Nesse, R.M. (Ed.), *Evolution and the Capacity for Commitment*. New York, NY: Russell Sage Press, 77–93.

Hollis, M. 1998. *Trust Within Reason*. Cambridge, UK: Cambridge University Press.

Hosmer, L.T. 1995. Trust: The Connecting Link between Organizational Theory and Philosophical Ethics. *Academy of Management Review*, 20(2), 379–403.

James, H.S., Jr. 2002. The Trust Paradox: A Survey of Economic Inquiries into the Nature of Trust and Trustworthiness. *Journal of Economic Behavior & Organization*, 47(3), 291–307.

Knack, S., Keefer, P. 1997. Does Social Capital have a Payoff? A Cross-Country Investigation. *Quarterly Journal of Economics*, 112(4), 1251–1288.

Knack, S., Zak, P.J. 2002. Building Trust: Public Policy, Interpersonal Trust, and Economic Development. *Supreme Court Economic Review*, 10, 91–107.

Knight, J. 1990. *Institutions and Social Conflict*. Cambridge, UK: Cambridge University Press.

Kollock, P. 1994. The Emergence of Exchange Structures: An Experimental Study of Uncertainty, Commitment, and Trust. *American Journal of Sociology*, 100(2), 313–345.

Lahno, B. 1995. Trust, Reputation, and Exit in Exchange Relationships. *The Journal of Conflict Resolution*, 39, 495–510.

Landa, J. 1981. A Theory of the Ethnically Homogenous Middleman Group: An Institutional Alternative to Contract Law. *Journal of Legal Studies*, 10, 349–362.

Landa, J. 1994. *Trust, Ethnicity, and Identity*. Ann Arbor, MI: University of Michigan Press.

Lane, C. 1998. Introduction: Theories and Issues in the Study of Trust. In: Lane, C., Bachmann, R. (Eds), *Trust Within the Between Organizations: Conceptual Issues and Empirical Applications*. Oxford: Oxford University Press, 1–30.

La Porta, R., Lopez-de-Silanes, F., Shleifer, A., Vishny, R.W. 1997. Trust in Large Organizations. *American Economic Review Papers and Proceedings*, 87(2), 333–338.

Lave, C.A., March, J.G. 1975. *An Introduction to Models in the Social Sciences*. New York, NY: Harper & Row, 1–84.

Leeson, P.T. 2008. Social Distance and Self-Enforcing Exchange. *Journal of Legal Studies*, 37, 161–188.

Levi, M. 1998. A State of Trust. In: Braithwaite, V., Levi, M. (Eds), *Trust and Governance*. New York, NY: Russell Sage, 77–101.

Lewis, J.D., Weigert, A. 1985. Trust as a Social Reality. *Social Forces*, 63, 967–985.

Luhmann, N. 1979. *Trust and Power: Two Works by Niklas Luhmann*. Translation of German Originals, Vertrauen (1968) and Macht (1975). Chichester: John Wiley.

Luhmann, N. 1988. Familiarity, Confidence, Trust: Problems and Alternatives. In: Gambetta, D. (Ed.), *Trust: Making and Breaking Co-operative Relations*. Oxford: Basil Blackwell, 94–107.

Macaulay, S. 1963. Non-Contractual Relations in Business: A Preliminary Study. *American Sociological Review*, 28(1), 55–67.

Maynard Smith, J. 1982. *Evolution and the Theory of Games*. Cambridge, UK: Cambridge University Press.

Maynard Smith, J., Price, G.R. 1973. The Logic of Animal Conflict. *Nature*, 246, 15–18.

Miller, A.H. 1974. Political Issues and Trust in Government: 1960–1970. *American Political Science Review*, 68, 951–972.

Milgrom, P., North, D.C., Weingast, B.R. 1990. The Role of Institutions in the Revival of Trade: The Law Merchant, Private Judges and the Champagne Fairs. *Economics and Politics*, 2(1), 1–23.

Milinski, M., Semmann, D., Krambeck, H.J. 2002. Reputation Helps Solve the Tragedy of the Commons. *Nature*, 415, 424–426.

Misztal, B.A. 1996. *Trust in Modern Societies*. Cambridge, MA: Polity Press.

Möllering, G. 2001. The Nature of Trust: From Georg Simmel to a Theory of Expectation, Interpretation and Suspension. *Sociology*, 35, 403–420.

Möllering, G. 2006. *Trust: Reason, Routine, Reflexivity*. Oxford: Elsevier.

Nickel, P.J., Vaesen, K. 2012. Risk and Trust. In: Roeser, S., Hillerbrand, R., Sandin, P., Peterson, M. (Eds), *Handbook of Risk Theory: Epistemology, Decision Theory, Ethics and Social Implications of Risk*. Dordrecht, Heidelberg, London, New York, NY: Springer, 856–876.

North, D.C. 1990. *Institutions, Institutional Change and Economic Performance*. Cambridge, UK: Cambridge University Press.

Nowak, M., Sigmund, K. 1998. The Dynamics of Indirect Reciprocity. *Journal of Theoretical Biology*, 194, 561–574.

Perelman, M. 1998. The Neglected Economics of Trust: The Bentham Paradox and Its Implications. *American Journal of Economics and Sociology*, 57(4), 381–389.

Popkin, S. 1981. Public Choice and Rural Development-Free Riders, Lemons, and Institutional Design. In: Russel, C., Nicholson, N. (Eds), *Public Choice and Rural Development*. Washington, DC: Resources for the Future, 43–80.

Poppo, L., Zenger, T. 2002. Do Formal Contracts and Relational Governance Function as Substitutes or Complements? *Strategic Management Journal*, 23, 707–725.

Powell, W.W., DiMaggio, P.J. 1991. *The New Institutionalism in Organizational Analysis*. Chicago, IL: University of Chicago Press.

Resnick, P., Zeckhauser, R. 2002. Trust Among Strangers in Internet Transactions: Empirical Analysis of eBay's Reputation System. *The Economics of Internet and E-Commerce*, 11, 127–157.

Ross, S. 1973. The Economic Theory of Agency: The Principle's Problem. *American Economic Review*, 63(2), 134–139.

Schotter, A. 1981. *The Economic Theory of Social Institutions*. Cambridge, UK, New York, NY: Cambridge University Press.

Shapiro, S.P. 1987. The Social Control of Impersonal Trust. *American Journal of Sociology*, 93(3), 623–658.

Siamwalla, A. 1978. Farmers and Middlemen: Aspects of Agricultural Marketing in Thailand. *Economic Bulletin for Asia and Pacific*, 39(1), 38–50.

Simmel, G. 1990. *The Philosophy of Money*. 2nd edition. London: Routledge. Translated from the 1907 German edition by Tom Bottomore and David Frisby. [Original ed. 1900].

Stolle, D. 1998. Bowling Together, Bowling Alone: The Development of Generalized Trust in Voluntary Associations. *Political Psychology*, 19(3), 497–525.

Stringham, E. 2002. The Emergence of the London Stock Exchange as a Self-Policing Club. *Journal of Private Enterprise*, 17(2), 1–19.

Sztompka, P. 1999. *Trust: A Sociological Theory*. Cambridge, UK: Cambridge University Press.

Trivers, R.L. 1971. The Evolution of Reciprocal Altruism. *Quarterly Review of Biology*, 46, 35–57.

Uslaner, E.M. 2002. *The Moral Foundations of Trust*. Cambridge, UK: Cambridge University Press.

Whitener, E.M., Brodt, S.E., Korsgaard, M.A., Werner, J.M. 1998. Managers as Initiators of Trust: An Exchange Relationship Framework for Understanding Managerial Trustworthy Behavior. *Academy of Management Review*, 23(3), 513–530.

Williamson, O.E. 1975. *Markets and Hierarchies*. New York, NY: Free Press.

Williamson, O.E. 1985. *The Economic Institutions of Capitalism: Firms, Markets, Relational Contracting*. New York, NY: Free Press.

Williamson, O.E. 1993. Calcultiveness, Trust, and Economic Organization. *Journal of Law and Economics*, 36, 453–486.

Yamagishi, T., Cook, K.S., Watabe, M. 1998. Uncertainty, Trust, and Commitment Formation in the United States and Japan. *American Journal of Sociology*, 104(1), 165–194.

Zucker, L.G. 1986. Production of Trust: Institutional Source of Economic Structure, 1840–1920. In: Staw, B.M., Cummings, L.L. (Eds), *Research in Organizational Behavior*, Vol. 8. Greenwich, CT: JAI Press, 53–111.

2 Theory

According to Möllering (2006), "Trust is a typical example of transitions between micro-level individual action and macro-level states of a system" (p. 15). Imagine a situation in which large economic interactions exist among rational self-interested agents. Trusting the interaction partners implies a problem because agents seeking to maximize their individual payoffs could destroy the collective benefits. Hence, after a number of interactions, the behavior of the remaining agents prevents them from trusting their interaction partners for bilateral benefits, leading to distrust. Thus, the state of trust in the economic system is the aggregated result of all the strategic choices made at the micro level (Güth and Kliemt, 2004).

I first explain this relationship by focusing on how economic agents' actions in micro-level interactions affect the macro-level state of trust.

In this domain, Kollock (1994) was among the first authors to conclude that the emergence of an exchange structure forms different macro-level trust phenomena when rational agents repeatedly interact at the local level. For example, buying a secondhand car is a case in point (Akerlof, 1970). In this exchange, the buyer has to trust the seller, as any advanced examination of the actual quality of the vehicle is impossible unless it has been driven for several months. As this case suggests, possible cheating behavior by sellers eliminates potential trusting behavior, even if contracts are concluded (because contracts are expensive and incomplete). In other words, a certain exchange structure gives rise to the strategic choices of rational agents and thereby to trust phenomena.

In sum, this study illustrates that trust is influenced by different exchange structures in local interactions. Based on the foregoing, this chapter extends this idea by considering the emergence of exchange structures in large interactions from an historical perspective (i.e., the evolution of trust in large exchange structures), thereby providing the foundation for exploring different interactive trust phenomena and formulating the co-evolving theory of exchange systems and trust.

Throughout economic history, transactional systems have evolved through three phases, namely barter, monetary, and Internet exchanges, which help draw general conclusions about the modern economy. Many institutional theorists have strived to understand the theoretical origins of economic phenomena. According to Dopfer (1986), "the historicity of economic phenomena must come into the theoretical picture" (p. 1007), leading to "explicit theories [being] tendered about the course of economic history" (Popper, 1945, p. 3).

In all but the earliest transaction system (i.e., barter), the emergence of exchange structures encouraged double defecting behaviors because of the presence of uncertainties, thereby serving to prevent trusting behavior in exchange processes. For example, an owner of silk wants to barter in order to receive a golden pot. Because both parties have specific knowledge about their own goods, defection should be straightforward. By contrast, the monetary system serves to alter the exchange structure, inducing one to act opportunistically because of the presence of money. Reconsider the secondhand car example. The seller may pursue exploitation to take advantage of the mutual benefits by seeking self-interest, whereas the buyer only places trust and waits for the outcome after payment has been made. Hence, the order of trust phenomena may appear spontaneously when large interactions are repeated under the different exchange structures of barter, monetary, and Internet.

In this chapter, in order to meet these demands, I elaborate on the fundamental issues that underlie the argument that trust is embedded in exchange, which could form co-evolving phenomena in response to the evolution of exchange systems. The general theory is developed in three stages. First, the basic connotations and problems of trust are presented. Second, the theories employed in previous economic studies about trust in exchange (e.g., TCT) are demonstrated as generally as possible, further enhancing our understanding of the trust paradox and its shortcomings. Third, by elaborating on the underpinning theory (i.e., the theory of the system of trust), the emergent exchange structures brought about by exchange systems are specified. In particular, I emphasize that trust in complex settings (i.e., interactive processes) is treated as a system that involves elements (e.g., agents, behaviors), interdependence, the micro-to-macro transition, and the macro-to-micro transition and that is influenced by forces acting upon agents and behaviors, namely the exchange structure. These theoretical points serve as the foundation for exploring interactive trust phenomena in exchange systems.

Exchange and trust

The concept of trust in economic exchange

Gambetta (1988) stated that trust is considered to exist when "the probability that the trustee will perform an action that is beneficial or at least not detrimental to us is high enough for us to consider engaging in some form of cooperation with him" (p. 217). In terms of expectation, Möllering (2001, p. 404) defined trust as "a state of favorable expectation regarding other individual actions and intentions". In what follows, this thesis does not merely follow the tradition of using expectation-based trust to explain the problem of trust in exchange (e.g., Simmel, 1990). Rather, I follow Coleman's (1990) definition of trust as a rational choice in "situations in which the risk one takes depends on the performance of another actor" (p. 91; see also Hosmer, 1995; Lane, 1998; Whitener *et al.*, 1998).

Although this definition does not consider trust in its natural environment, situation-based trust implies that rational agents involved interactively place trust through several methods in various situations. This approach has led to the formation of different concepts of trust in previous studies, such as expectation-based trust, reason-based trust, calculation-based trust, and imitation-based trust (see Table 2.1).

When situations are not characterized by defecting behavior, trust is considered to be an extravagance. However, defection has many opportunities to arise in real life because of our less-than-perfect circumstances owing to asymmetric information, contractual incompleteness, and so on. Hence, this point illustrates the trust paradox in economic exchange, namely how rational agents can constrain their self-interest in order to trust each other in exchange.

Therefore, the fundamental problem of whether rational agents are willing to achieve bilateral benefits is not that placing trust is a matter of blindness and indifference that is randomly chosen in the interaction. Instead, it is that agents rationally selecting trust rely on conditions under which abnormal actions may violate trust being placed.

Table 2.1 Rational choice approaches and trust studies

Expectation-based trust	**Reason-based trust**
e.g., Coleman (1990), Gambetta (1988), Elsner and Heinrich (2009), Elsner and Schwardt (2014)	e.g., Hardin (2006), Möllering (2006), Hollis (1998)
Calculation-based trust	**Imitation-based trust**
e.g., Williamson (1985), James (2002)	See Chapter 4, section "Emergence of trust: A model of imitation"

Coleman's (1990) contribution to the expectation-based trust subcategory is often emphasized, because he directly considered the nature of trust in order to provide the foundation for trust studies that adopt RCT. Coleman (1982) based his theory of the system of trust on the notion of expectation, which arises under risks, stating the trust is taken as a "part of a larger theory of social action" (p. 281). Further, from the perspective of behavioral dynamics, "Trust is a typical example of transitions between micro-level individual action and macro-level states of a system" (Möllering, 2006, p. 15).

Further, Coleman's (1990) attempt to explain the relevance of trust to expectation was based on an estimated measure of agents' chances of winning and losing. For example, if the potential gain is represented by M, potential loss by N, and the probability of expecting a partner to be trustworthy by $p(0 < p < 1)$, agents place trust in the interaction partners when $Mp > N(1 - p)$ (Möllering, 2006).

Finally, Coleman (1990) introduced expectation-based trust into his linear system of behavior, arguing that full trust is lacking in large interactive systems because trust is strongly affected by the combination of price and participants' interests, which unpredictably alters the long-term equilibria of systems.

Coleman's works on expectation-based trust support our tautological point on trust as embedded in exchange because of its expected nature. Although Coleman (1982, 1990) failed to explain, or even emphasize, how this subjective probability (i.e., expectation) is derived, it is reasonable for a purposive actor to use any information available in order to predict the actions of interaction partners. Hence, expectation-based trust comprises the costly matter of searching for and analyzing information, which suggests that reducing costs is a premise of this category of trust.

In this area, Elsner and Heinrich (2009) were notable for taking trust as a "commodity" that emerges and co-evolves from expectation, laying a new platform for future studies of trust. For details about this theory, refer to Elsner and Heinrich (2009) and Elsner and Schwardt (2014).

Unlike Coleman (1982, 1990), Hardin (2006) highlighted the function of "reason" in current studies of trust, stating that "I trust someone if I have reason to believe it will be in that person's interest to be trustworthy in the relevant way at the relevant time" (p. 19). Hardin's work categorized reason-based trust into three relationships: agent A trusts B because A forms judgments logically with respect to X. For instance, in an exchange, I trust you because you are my friend and valuable to me, and you have a good reputation, and thus I take account of your interests when deciding on my degree of trust. Note, however, that "this does not mean that your interests trump mine for me" (Hardin, 2006, p. 19). Rather, it means that "you have an interest in fulfilling my trust" (Hardin, 2006, p. 3).

Hardin (2006) regarded that player A may encapsulate B's interest in trusting for various reasons. Among these, the three most common mechanisms are "ongoing beneficial relationship," "social embeddedness" (e.g., being a friend), and "reputation," confirming the importance of the role of relationships in trust processes. Following this logic, our society is a network that supports underlying trust (Hardin, 2006). Indeed, we can consider the effect of encapsulated interest on the situation of trust as similar to that "where the risk one takes depends on the performance of another actor" (Coleman, 1990, p. 91). In other words, I encapsulate your interests, but my partner has opportunities to act opportunistically.

Trust is endowed in a calculative sense because of the existence of transaction costs. Based on TCT, agents should rationally believe that their "exchange partner will act opportunistically" (Bradach and Eccles, 1989, p. 104). Thus, in practice various mechanisms such as executing contracts are used to retain the confidence of the involved parties and safeguard transactions to avoid agents perceiving their partners as untrustworthy (Bigley and Pearce, 1998). However, controlling opportunism incurs higher costs, suggesting that trust building is rational under certain circumstances, especially when parties can perceive the trustworthiness of one another.

Williamson (1993) cautioned against only viewing trust as a calculative base and argued that trust has a non-calculative meaning, which influences personal relationships. Nevertheless, this caveat accepts the calculative sense of trust. Similarly, Gulati (1995) and Dyer (2000) found that unless the cost of avoiding opportunism is lower in inter-firm alliances, the contract can supersede trust and take advantage of its enforcement to reduce opportunistic behavior. Indeed, according to Möllering (2006), "Trust is more effective than legal contracts in minimizing transaction costs" (p. 27).

Calculation-based trust, which aims to minimize transaction costs according to Williamson's theory, faces the same risk of opportunists exploiting the trust placed, and thus the performance of the trustor is dependent on the future actions of the other party. Note, however, that calculation-based trust is not limited to a calculated, rational choice under all circumstances. That is, when economic agents perceive the trustworthiness of interaction partners, higher transaction costs are only one reason for placing trust. In other words, rationality depends on expectation, reason, and calculation when dealing with defection under uncertainty, which leads us to extend this idea through the elaboration of imitation-based trust.

The idea of imitation-based trust in economics rarely receives close attention. While it may seem to be an unusual concept at first glance, many phenomena allow it to exist in practice. For example, one of your friends is more likely to trust another friend, which in turn makes it more likely that you will trust his or her friends. In this sense, you are imitating his or her trust. Similarly, when a bank run occurs, regardless of your confidence in the bank, you may be more tempted to withdraw your savings (you are imitating others' distrust in this case).

Therefore, trust is a matter of imitation under certain circumstances. This argument is also supported by one of the basic assumptions of behavioral economics: *bounded rationality*. Because agents are often restricted by various factors (e.g., imperfect information), rationality is bounded, which limits how they behave. In this context, when individuals are uncertain, they are willing to follow the lead of others (Kandori *et al.*, 1993; Weibull, 1998; Nowak *et al.*, 2004; Fudenberg and Imhof, 2008).

The same point underlies the organizational observation made by Barrear and Buskens (2007) that "both imitation and learning have effects on trust situations and that these effects depend on uncertainties for the trustor" (p. 367). Orléans (1998) extended this point on imitation to the idea of collective efficiency, arguing that if imitation works, there is a force for trust or distrust and thus the promotion of collective efficiency. In conclusion, imitation-based trust occurs when faced with a risky situation and when performance is dependent on the future actions of others.

The prevailing viewpoint in the studies mentioned above is that if defection exists, trust may be a rational choice. However, rational agents can also include such matters as expectation, reason, calculation, and imitation when deciding on their levels of trust. Hence, trust is not a taken-for-granted matter, thus explaining the existence of the trust paradox in economic exchange. However, when certain conditions are satisfied, agents will rationally trust one another.

This explanation is re-emphasized in Chapter 4, which describes the necessary conditions for the emergence of trust in these contexts. Specifically, rational agents base their decision-making on trust on expectation, reason, calculation, and imitation.

Before we proceed, however, I introduce certain economic theories in the exchange domain in order to support our understanding of the exchange–trust relationship, which further serves as a foundation for elaborating on the theory of the system of trust. Note that two of the main economic exchange theories, namely TCT and agency theory, do not focus on trust phenomena in the interactive process of exchange. These are reviewed next.

Trust in current exchange theories

This section starts with a discussion of the foundations and applications of TCT and agency theory before elaborating on the underpinning theory in this study. In these studies of trust in exchange, opportunism is a key assumption, while prevailing theories commonly lack an interactive context in a large population. Thus, combining these two points allows us to jointly extend the body of research to formulate a co-evolving theory of trust and exchange systems through an evolutionary paradigm.

TCT

TCT is grounded on the theoretical framework for the interpretation of trust problems in exchange (see Williamson, 1993, 1996). Extensions and further applications of the theory have been presented by Barney and Hansen (1994), Cummings and Bromiley (1996), and Bigley and Pearce (1998).

The basic assumption of all research on trust in exchange is that rational agents act opportunistically (Möllering, 2006). Opportunism can be defined as "the opposite of trust" (Barney and Hansen, 1994, p. 176), or "acting to promote one's welfare by the taking advantage of a trust extended by an individual, group, or society as a whole" (Rose, 2011, p. 21). According to Williamson (1985), opportunism is "self-interest seeking with guile" (p. 47). Because opportunism is presupposed to exploit the trust in exchange, its role underpins the prerequisite of trust, where "the risk one takes depends on the performance of another actor" (Coleman, 1990, p. 91). This further implies that "there is an element of trust in every transaction" (Arrow, 1973, p. 24) because opportunism lasts forever, even though its degree varies.

TCT recognizes that the rationality of agents in exchange relationships is bounded and thereby supports effective forms of governance (e.g., market forces, hierarchical authority) for reducing uncertainty and transaction costs. According to TCT, ordinary costs include expenditure on searching for information, bargaining, enforcing the cooperation, and other things that occur in the economic exchange. However, several costs are relevant to the relation between opportunism and trust even if they are considered to be necessary expenditures. For example, contracting aims to avoid opportunistic behavior but such cost would be saved if trust were instead used. Therefore, it can be inferred that trust may be able to minimize transaction costs. However, the paradox of trust arises once again: why do rational agents constrain self-interest even though opportunism exists?

From a game-theoretical perspective, rational agents exploit trust in a one-shot PD game (i.e., exchange), in addition to a repeated situation when they expect to interact in the future. However, exchange often happens between strangers in a society characterized by more one-shot situations with strangers. If the transaction costs that result from the enforcement costs incurred by, for example, executing contracts are lower, agents are willing to accept them in order to reduce risk. If and only if they are higher, placing trust is rational. We can thus use exchange to explain this issue (see Figure 2.1).

In Figure 2.1, each column and row represents two agents with two actions, namely cooperation and defection, who attempt to finish the transaction but

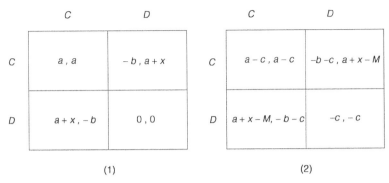

Figure 2.1 Exchange (1), and exchange with a contract (2) ($0 < b < a < a + x, 0 < c, M$).

face two situations. As shown in (1), if neither agent in the one-shot situation of exchange enforces the contract, the best strategy is defection. (2) suggests that although the contract executed adds punishment M (including c) to the agent with the defecting agent, it will also add cost c to the payoffs of mutual cooperation if the interaction partner cooperates and to the payoffs of one-sided cooperation. Hence, when one (cooperating) party knows that his or her counterpart will cooperate, he or she will take a risk trusting without executing the contract by calculating the payoffs when cost c is much higher (i.e., $(a - c) < a$) (see Chapter 4, section "The foundation of the emergence of trust in behavioral interdependence" for more details).

This idea was empirically accepted by Cummings and Bromiley (1996) in an organizational context. These authors insisted that if the trustworthiness of a firm can be perceived, trust is rationally used to reduce transaction costs. However, how agents can perceive the trustworthiness of their interaction partner is unclear. Intuitively, agents need to base their perception on certain factors such as signal, "shadow of the future" (repeated action), reputation, and so forth.

Attention in the discussion of TCT above is paid to two key points. First, "opportunism and bounded rationality are the key behavioral assumptions on which transaction cost economics relies" (Williamson, 1993, p. 458). Second, taken together, two assumptions suggest that trust is embedded in exchange: (i) risk always exists because the agents in exchange are "intendedly rational, but only limitedly so" (Simon, 1957, p. 24) and (ii) risk always exists because agents pursue self-interest (i.e., opportunism).

Agency theory

Agency theory (also known as principal–agent theory) has been referred to as the earliest mode of economic interaction (see Ross, 1973). Nevertheless,

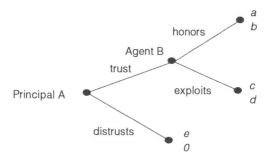

Figure 2.2 The trust game ($c < 0 < e < b < a < d$).

Shapiro (1987) turned scholarly attention to the study of impersonal trust by employing the social organization of agency as a tool to examine the dilemmas of agency, clarifying that trust is an underlying setting embedded in a series of discussions.

The trust problem can be perceived when the principal hires an agent to deal with a task on his or her behalf in return for a reward (Jensen and Meckling, 1976; Möllering, 2006). This problem arises because "situations in which the risk one takes depends on the performance of another actor" (Coleman, 1990, p. 91) are created, where an agent is presumed to maximize self-profits by exploiting the trustworthiness of the principal, raising moral hazard (Arrow, 1970). The agency problem is thus crucial for studying the importance of trust in exchange relationships (e.g., between owners and managers or banks and depositors; Ross, 1973).

The trust problem under agency theory can be presented by a simple trust game (see Figure 2.2). In this game, principal *A* decides whether to trust agent *B* to perform an action, while agent *B* determines the allocation of profits. If principal *A* distrusts agent *B*, they will receive the values *e* and 0, respectively. If principal *A* trusts agent *B* and if agent *B* honors this trust-worthiness, they will obtain values *a* and *b*, respectively; however, if agent *B* exploits this trustworthiness, they will receive values *c* and *d*, respectively. The final outcome for the trust game, from a game-theoretical perspective, is that principal *A* distrusts agent *B* to honor his or her trustworthiness when they face uncertainties (i.e., a backward induction), thereby creating the "trust dilemma." Solving this dilemma involves changing the preferences of players (e.g., by writing an explicit or implicit contract) as well as repeating the interaction (James, 2002).

Consider one of the solutions (i.e., writing an explicit contract) as an example. The trust problem here displays hidden information, hidden action, and hidden intention (Arrow, 1985; Eisenhardt, 1989; Möllering, 2006). The conventional way in which to reduce these is to sign an explicit contract.

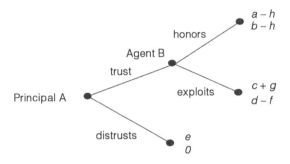

Figure 2.3 The trust game with a contract ($c < 0 < e < b < a < d, 0 < h, f, g$).

Each party will thus have to pay costs h to obtain payoffs – $(a - h)$ and $(b - h)$ for principal A and agent B, respectively (see Figure 2.3). Meanwhile, the contract will lay punishment f on agent B and provide compensation g to principal A if the agent chooses to exploit this trust. Hence, for the condition of trust between principal A and agent B to be reached, the payoffs of exploitation must be less than those of trust, namely $(d - f) < (b - h)$. In other words, principal A rationally knows that agent B has no interest in exploiting his or her trustworthiness.

Indeed, the question under focus in agency theory is identical to that in game theory apart from the mathematical formulation. Therefore, using game theory to shed light on agency theory is suitable for understanding the problem of trust. In the following section, I employ this method to address a crucial theory, namely the theory of the system of trust, in order to help analyze interactive trust phenomena in exchange systems and thereby achieve a co-evolving theory of trust and exchange systems.

Co-evolving trust and exchange systems: The implication of a theory of the system of trust

Exchange and trust may co-evolve historically, but mainstream economics studies of trust have overlooked this historical trend (e.g., TCT and agency theory), focusing on individual episodes rather than on the evolutionary process. Furthermore, stories of exchange and trust are presumed as having an empirical relation (i.e., cause and effect), not a dynamic process that expresses that trust is one of the dynamic outcomes. Hence, solving the problems above is not only about understanding how historical changes in exchange have affected trust, but also about presenting and drawing conclusions on the characteristics (e.g., emergence, evolution, and stability of trust) in each exchange system in order to achieve a co-evolving theory of trust and exchange systems.

In my analysis of studies of trust in previous sections, I proceeded from the concept of trust in exchange, recognized as a rational choice in "situations in which the risk one takes depends on the performance of another actor" (Coleman, 1990, p. 91) to current exchange theories. I next apply this concept to two problems of trust in static exchange in the form of game-theoretical structures (see Figures 2.1 and 2.2). I consider trust in a largely interactive transactional context (e.g., barter, monetary, and Internet) by seeing the system of trust as composed of components, namely the "purposive actions of individual actors, deciding to place or withdraw trust or to break or keep trust; the micro-to-macro transition through which these actions combine to bring about behavior of system; and the macro-to-micro transition through which some state of the system modifies the decisions of individual actors to place trust and to be trustworthy" (Coleman, 1990, p. 175) (see Figure 2.4).

The key factor of the theory of the system of trust is understanding how different exchange systems organize or alter these components in this system of trust in order to produce distinct interactive trust characteristics (e.g., emergence, evolution, and stability) during micro-to-macro and macro-to-micro transitions. In the following, I start by providing a detailed description of the system of trust to illustrate that trust is an interactive phenomenon of exchange, characterized as micro-to-macro and macro-to-micro transitions in the system of trust formed by interdependent actions by economic agents who try to pursue self-interest in exchange.

Systems of trust: Elements, interdependences, and micro-to-macro/macro-to-micro transitions

Real market interactions are characterized by the direct or indirect interdependence of the agents involved (Elsner, 2013). Under these circumstances, the behaviors of rational individuals vary interdependently over time, leading to certain results.

The importance of an interdependent context involving trust becomes explicit when noticeable interactive phenomena in the market (e.g., panic buying and bank runs) emerge, aggregate, and explode. In these processes, it is important to understand that various behaviors are involved that together interdependently modify the trust in a system and that exchange is inevitably influenced by the trust in each exchange, while exchange indeed alters trust in a dynamic process.

The foregoing implies that the explanatory trust within exchange systems can be framed by *constraining a set of economic individuals, a set of actions, and a set of rules as a subsystem: a system of trust* (Coleman, 1990) provided

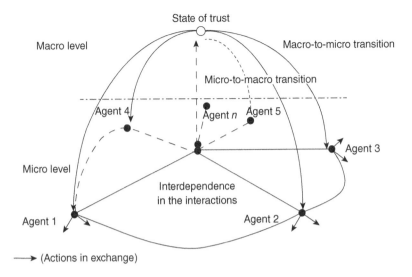

Figure 2.4 System of trust.

the interactive context (i.e., interdependence) is considered in general. In this sense, the framework under which individuals choose actions that affect trust is defined as a process that interdependently influences the behaviors of all parties and that is sparked by the emergence of and change to these behaviors. When friendly-trusting behavior emerges and interdependently aggregates, this increases the trust in the system; on the contrary, when this behavior fails to emerge, defecting behavior arises. Hence, an interdependent transitive process in the system must be described explicitly in studies of trust because this entails a theory on how the utilization of interactive force promotes trust overall. With the help of this framework, this study extends the focus to interactive trust phenomena in the system by addressing two research questions. First, how do the emergence, evolution, and stability of trust occur in this system in which economic individuals interdependently behave to maximize their utilities? Second, how do exchange systems influence these components in a system of trust? By referring to these questions, a systematic transition process of trust in the system is explained and the possible matters that guide this interactive process revealed. Before going further, however, an interpretation of these components in a system of trust is necessary.

Individuals

First, social and economic phenomena are the outcomes of human activities. Traditional behavioral assumptions in economics state that individuals are animals that seek to maximize profits by pursuing self-interest, so-called "self-interest seeking with guile" (Williamson, 1975, p. 47). In brief, if agents' actions in exchange can give rise to higher payoffs, the incentive of self-interest works to maximize utility by pursuing it. Therefore, individuals in an exchange process are opportunists who pursue their maximized utility based on TCT and agency theory, as mentioned earlier, of which a key assumption is opportunism, which arises as either *contracting costs* in the transaction or *moral hazard* in the agency relationship (Arrow, 1970). However, this argument is incorrect because people are not always maximizing and their behaviors are restricted by various incentive structures (e.g., PD) when deciding how to best respond to their partner's choices. Our concern for individuals in the system of trust thus is that rational ones interdependently engage in exchange.

Behaviors

Second, since defection, "the opposite of trust" (Barney and Hansen, 1994, p. 176), exists in exchange, leading to "situations in which the risk one takes depends on the performance of another actor" (Coleman, 1990, p. 91), trust is a "commodity" of action (i.e., a strategy) in exchange (Axelrod and Hamilton, 1981; Kreps *et al*., 1982; Williamson, 1983; Tullock, 1985; Kollock, 1994; Nooteboom, 1996; Hirshleifer, 1999; Elsner and Heinrich, 2009). In this respect, Coleman (1990) divided trust into the asymmetric and symmetric relations that occur in social interactions (see Table 2.2). In this sense, the choices of individuals in the system of trust that appear in transactions can be simply outlined as two actions, namely trust or not to trust (although a more precise treatment is discussed in the section "Trust in

Table 2.2 Incentives for trust in asymmetric and symmetric relations

Choice of action	*Incentives in asymmetric relation*	*Additional incentives in mutual relation*
Keeping or breaking trust	Benefits lost because other will not place trust in the future	Other, as trustee, will break trust if I do
Placing or not placing trust	Expectation of gain (pG) from others' trustworthy action is greater than expectation of loss ($[1 - p]L$)	p is increased by one's sanctioning power in breaking trust if other does; G is increased by future benefits from other as trustee

Source: Coleman (1990, p. 178).

the evolution of exchange systems: Interdependence structures and populations in the system of trust" below).

For simplicity, here I have elaborated on the core points about individuals and behaviors in the system of trust. Next, the micro-to-macro and macro-to-micro transitions of trust in the system are explained. First, interdependence as a foundation to underpin the micro-to-macro and macro-to-micro transitions of trust is discussed. Second, from an evolutionary perspective (i.e., the evolutionary approach introduced in Chapter 3), the importance of interdependent structures in transitions of trust is illustrated. This serves as a foundation for understanding the argument of this study that the emergence of interactive structures in exchange systems is different, which is a reason for the distinct interactive trust phenomena (e.g., emergence, evolution, stability) in transactions.

Interdependence forms

Interactions among economic agents are characterized by interdependence. To illustrate this point, imagine two scenarios for a buyer and a seller, who are attempting to agree a deal. In the first scenario, their interests are in conflict: the buyer is willing to agree the deal at a lower price and instead the seller wants to sell the commodities at a higher price. Under such a circumstance, they engage in several rounds of negotiation before the exchange is achieved. Of course, in this process each person will attempt to protect self-interest through communication, although they may consider the interests of the interaction partner if this deal is crucial to both parties. Ultimately, a common price may be agreed to solve this problem. In this case, interdependence between the buyer and seller is related to the environment (i.e., the market) and independent of the actions of the interaction partners.

In the second scenario, their interests are consonant (repeated exchange). In this situation, both want to form a long-term relationship to reduce risk. Neither is more concerned about the factor price; indeed, they rather rely on the past actions of the interaction partner. If benevolent behaviors occurred in the past, a partnership could be formed. Combining these settings shows that, regardless of whether the interests of the interacting parties correspond or conflict, their actions are interdependent.

To extend this point, these two scenarios simply suggest that the economic system is an interdependent system and interdependence can help reveal the micro-to-macro and macro-to-micro transitions of trust when trust is recognized as a *choice* in interactive exchange.

When trust is placed into the interactive context, a common logical consequence must be followed, namely explaining interdependence forms. Interdependence in social behavior among individuals presents three types

(Friedman, 1977). In the first one, named structural interdependence, each individual, when deciding to choose an action, considers the interaction partner's actions to a lesser degree and rather relies on the environment (Coleman, 1990), as shown in the first scenario. Similarly, under expectation-based trust, people expect to trust the interaction partner, but trust is more likely to be deduced from the impersonal environment. For example, in a job market, managers often regard the average level of employees as a basis for judging the capabilities of new applicants.

The second form of interdependence is behavioral interdependence. This form is described in situations in which the behaviors of individuals are conditional on one another because one's performance is dependent on the future actions of the other. Game theory presents this form of interdependence by using various games such as PD, Trust, and Snowdrift games. According to these games, the outcomes of the interdependent process will produce certain equilibria through human rationality and common behaviors. These games also provide distinct incentives for participants in the interactive structure, such as two-sided defection in PD and one-sided defection in Trust games. In some senses, behavioral interdependence is decidedly constrained by the interactive structures that involve incentives (i.e., interdependent structures).

The third form of interdependence is evolutionary interdependence, which emphasizes the processes and outcomes of various interacting behaviors among a population. For example, evolutionary interdependence is more likely to occur in interactions in which individuals follow those that display the best behaviors (i.e., imitation) even if they do not interact. Put differently, behavioral interdependence reflects a constrained process in an individual-to-individual context, while evolutionary interdependence rather describes one in a collective-to-individual or a one-to-collective context.

This study is limited to the second and third forms of interdependence, which were overlooked by Coleman (1990) in his theory of the system of trust. In Chapter 4, individuals are examined under behavioral and evolutionary interdependences in order to assess how trust emerges in interactive exchange contexts. In Chapter 5, the evolution and stability of trust are mainly considered according to evolutionary interdependence. To describe interactive trust phenomena in interdependence, the evolutionary approach is applied; however, before applying this approach, an important basis for the analysis must be explained, namely interdependence structures.

Interdependence structures: Symmetric and asymmetric contexts from an evolutionary perspective

To understand the basic argument that underlies the co-evolving theory of exchange systems and trust as well as to explain how exchange systems affect the components in the system of trust, it is necessary to describe the extent to which matters affect the micro-to-macro and macro-to-micro transitions of trust in evolutionary interdependence from a more theoretical orientation. We are lacking knowledge on the elusive evolutionary approach, including its biological background and hypothesis. In this sense, this section focuses on the structures of interdependence from an evolutionary perspective, which serves as a foundation that stresses the importance of interdependent structures in evolutionary analysis.

Traditional economic and social studies have represented different forms of interdependence by using a matrix (i.e., interdependent or interactive structures) that includes two agents, each of whom have two actions, yielding four combinations and behavioral outcomes (Von Neumann and Morgenstern, 1944; Rusbult and Van Lange, 2003). These simple matrix patterns are helpful to describe how agents affect one another in social interactions. At this basic level, matrix patterns can be seen as a miniature pictorial representation of interdependence, influencing emergence, evolution, and stability, especially when they are repeated.

The foundations of matrix patterns are interpreted in the section "Trust in the evolution of exchange systems: Interdependence structures and populations in the system of trust". However, the evolutionary approach is more concerned with whether these matrix patterns are symmetric or asymmetric, namely whether interdependence represents a symmetric or an asymmetric context by classifying them through their roles and behaviors.

The symmetric structure of interdependence is the simplest one. In this structure, all individual roles and behaviors are the same and they all derive from a single population. In a biological context, simple cases include lions fighting to obtain food and male chimpanzees battling to breed (Gaunersdorfer *et al.*, 1991), whereas in a social context, one good example is of new applicants competing to obtain a new job. If this setting is considered according to evolutionary interdependence (by using the evolutionary approach), the evolutionary process is pushed further by using a linear differential system (i.e., replicator dynamic equations; see Chapter 3), as is familiar to economists. Then, it follows there may be a stable state (SS) at the end of the evolutionary process (see Chapter 5).

By contrast, the asymmetric structure is one in which individual behaviors and roles differ in interactions, while both parties are also from different populations. It is widely accepted that in economic interactions that involve at least two people with different roles from different populations, the asymmetric case is much more pronounced and frequent, such as the male–female, worker–queen, and buyer–seller contexts (Gaunersdorfer *et al.*, 1991). Maynard Smith (1982) empirically established how the asymmetric context brings about a distinct proliferation of evolutionary processes compared with the symmetric one. One of the differences based on the evolutionary approach, compared with the symmetric context, comes about because the evolutionary process is characterized by a double linear differential system with asymptotic stability (Selten, 1980), which thus generates two replicator equations for the two roles (see Chapter 5, section "Micro-to-macro transition of trust in exchange systems: Trust in different interactive structures and populations").

The different characteristics of such structures (e.g., double differential systems in the asymmetric context) change the evolutionary processes, which becomes a point with which to consider the micro-to-macro and macro-to-micro transitions of trust.

Micro-to-macro and macro-to-micro transitions of trust

The last part elaborated on the form and structure of interdependence as a main component of the system of trust for a process through which the choices of economic individuals interdependently affect trust. In this part, I affirm this point by classifying trust into two transitions that include three interactive trust phenomena: emergence, evolution, and stability. Although this treatment for studying trust in complex settings is simple, it offers a direct reflection on the expected outcomes, as this thesis explores exchange systems that lead to distinct interactive trust phenomena.

The empirical specification of these two transitions of trust was put forward by Coleman (1990). This author stated that the micro-to-macro system of trust is a *forward* process in which the interdependent organization of behaviors at the micro level further brings about trusting behavior in the system. By contrast, the macro-to-micro system of trust is a *backward* process in which the formed behavior of the system reversely adjusts the decision to place trust in the individual at the micro level. For simplicity, in order to translate these points from an abstract sense into a specific one, two transitions are presented here (a detailed introduction of these concepts is provided later).

The *emergence of trust* is a premise, or a starting point, of the dynamic process in the system of trust that refers to emergent trusting behavior in the whole system. According to this premise, the amount of trusting behavior increases in exchange. Recalling the discussions on interdependence, the emergence of trust is an outcome for which economic individuals interdependently (i.e., behavioral and evolutionary interdependences) place trust in an interdependent structure. This implies that the generation of trust requires a combination of forms and structures of interdependence to promote it jointly. This principle is systematically discussed in Chapter 4.

The *evolution of trust* is described as a movement in the frequencies of trusting behaviors in the system over time. This movement is an identical process to the micro-to-macro transition that combines individual behaviors with the state of the system. In other words, this process increases the likelihood that a certain behavior will dominate (i.e., one played by more or even all individuals). This increase raises the question about what makes a certain behavior (e.g., trust) dominate, as discussed in Chapter 5. Before elaborating on this issue, however, it is called evolutionary interdependence here.

The *stability of trust* is the extent to which an outcome from the macro-to-micro stabilizing process of trust is achieved because of trusting behavior first dominating another in the evolutionary process and thus becoming the behavior of the system, adjusting emergence and evolution and once again reinforcing its dominance. This is a general process for stability. However, the principles for predicting whether a behavior will be stable and where depend on the context (see Chapter 5).

The explanation of emergence, evolution, and stability aims to illustrate interactive phenomena in the macro-to-micro and micro-to-macro transitions in the system of trust in order to explain the core points of this study after elaborating on the elements and interdependence of the trust system. Further, the relationship between dynamic exchange and interactive trust phenomena in the system of trust is open.

Trust in the evolution of exchange systems: Interdependence structures and populations in the system of trust

Ever since Georg Simmel's book *The Philosophy of Money* in 1907 (Simmel, 1990), the influence of exchange on trust has been used to underpin the effects of economic growth. More recent contributions by Kollock (1994), Skaggs (1998), and others have used economic experiments to show how the emergence of exchange structures co-evolves with trust phenomena. In all these studies, exchange and its evolving patterns are recognized as either a foundation or a cause of changing trust if individuals are matched at the local level. However, this section argues that special outcomes may arise when considering trust in large populations in evolving exchange structures (i.e., interdependent structures).

This section presumes that trust is a subsystem in barter, money, and Internet economies in which individuals interdependently act in a large interaction, but are constrained by the distinct emergence of exchange patterns, possibly forming various interactive phenomena of trust (e.g., evolution and stability). In line with the descriptions of the system of trust, rather than extending the reasons for the evolution of transition economies, I explore the consequences after these transition economies have formed, narrowing the views toward the emergence of exchange structures in different ones.

To obtain a clearer characterization, the analysis of the emergence of interdependent structures is presented by using game theory. The analysis presented in this section shows that a symmetric structure across homogeneous matches results whenever individuals interact in a barter economy. This finding captures the characteristic in the barter economy of symmetric wants in all good matches (Engineer, 2001). With this feature, each individual is endowed with two roles simultaneously, namely buyer and seller. Therefore, individuals have the same roles and behaviors in exchange (i.e., symmetric structures), whereas an asymmetric structure across heterogeneous matches emerges when money intervenes. With this change, roles and behaviors are divided according to the position in each interaction: one is a buyer, which means that the other is a seller. Compared with monetary exchange, Internet exchange adds enforcements into the interactive process, which is simply taken as an asymmetric structure with punishment.

Thus, the analysis presented in this section aims to confirm that economic systems are interdependent. Yet, the emergence of interdependent structures in exchange systems could affect and give rise to different trust phenomena considering the micro-to-macro and macro-to-micro transitions of trust.

To demonstrate the emergence of interdependent structures, the remainder of this section proceeds as follows. First, knowledge about bartering, barter matches, and the barter economy is elaborated on to understand why the emergence of interactive structures is symmetric. Second, by using a similar logic, we talk about money, money matches, and the monetary economy, compared with the barter economy, to understand the function of the intervention of money, which changes the exchange structure in the barter economy into an asymmetric one. Finally, by combining these two transition economies, the characteristics of Internet exchange are defined as an asymmetric structure with punishment. All these exchanges help explain that evolving exchange systems bring about distinct interdependent structures in the system of trust.

Barter and trust

For young children, swapping toys with friends is a usual way in which to achieve mutual satisfaction. The process is created because children have insufficient pocket money to buy all the toys they desire. In this situation, using what you have to swap with your friends is rational. If money had not been invented, this type of exchange system would have continued because of the human instinct to satisfy needs. Therefore, bartering did not vanish because of human nature, even though the habit of using money has developed.

Bartering is an early type of exchange. In ancient times, so-called "silent trade" (or silent bartering) was popular. The common setting of these trades

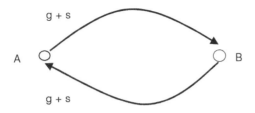

Figure 2.5 Barter exchange (Coleman, 1990, p. 21).

can be described as a structure (see Figure 2.5), where two agents with the "double coincidence of wants" (Edgeworth, 1881) directly exchange one good for other goods without a medium of exchange such as money (O'Sullivan and Sheffrin, 2003).

Bartering has advantages and disadvantages. On the positive side, it can operate even if the currency is unstable, thus providing a basic function for an economy undergoing harsh conditions. For example, the recent barter systems in some countries (e.g., Russia, Ukraine, Slovakia, Slovenia) have sustained the national economy. In this vein, Russia reported that its barter economy accounted for 60 percent of GDP in 1998 (Johnson *et al.*, 1997). By contrast, one of the main shortcomings of bartering is searching for a double coincidence of wants. For bartering to work between any two individuals, one person's need must be the other's good. Further, both parties need to have enough goods that the other wants, especially when the goods cannot be divided up. If bartering fails to be achieved, both parties should worry about the costs of goods, as they have to be stored, thus incurring storage costs as well as searching or sunk costs in the next exchange.

In a barter economy, little attention has been paid to a fundamental problem, namely trust. Bartering creates trust problems in two ways. First, although individuals can trade with one another, the limitations of bartering mean that the double coincidence of wants is rarely achieved. As the barter economy extends, it should develop one-to-many relationships to overcome the difficulty of direct one-to-one exchange. For example, individual *A* needs the goods of *B*, but individual *B* is bartering with *C*. It makes sense to individual *A* that a promise is agreed to move the goods of individual *C* in the near future under a precondition of immediately owning the goods of individual *B*. This process suggests that the whole network turns into a credit network (see Figure 2.6). Yet, this process brings about a basic "situation of trust in which the risk one takes depends on the performance of another actor" (Coleman, 1990, p. 91).

Second, before beginning to barter, people have to make a pre-commitment that the merchandise exchanged is of good quality to avert the

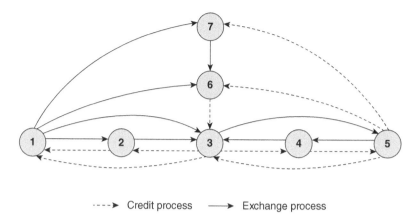

---▶ Credit process   ⟶ Exchange process

Figure 2.6 Credit networks in the barter economy.

suspicion of defection, as both parties possess specific knowledge about their goods. In this sense, the asymmetric information from the goods themselves generates a trust problem. For example, if a person barters his or her lamb with another person's golden pot, the latter might worry if the lamb has any pre-existing weaknesses (e.g., health issues, problems with legal status), while the former might worry if the golden pot has structural problems (e.g., mixed with iron, lead, and so on).

This study focuses on the second problem of trust brought about by bartering. The first issue refers to structured interactions in the network, which is partly mentioned in Chapter 6, where I argue that this is a main force to trigger varieties of changes in trust in the system over time.

Barter matches: Symmetric structure – two-sided PD across homogeneous matches

There is a universal symmetric coincidence of wants in all barter matches (Engineer, 2001). Yet, it is also widely verified that rational agents act opportunistically in exchange (Möllering, 2006), as elaborated on in Adam Smith's (1776) *The Wealth of Nations*, who noted that greed and self-interest are at the heart of all types of economic exchanges (in my argument, this is incomplete). I argue that possible defection and the symmetric character of the barter economy are unattached at first glance but come together in continuous bartering. In view of this, a possible convincing explanation is that people aim to either satisfy their needs or pursue self-interest in a certain incentive structure. For example, they may provide high-quality goods or low-quality goods. This means that "double needs" are possibly

Player 2

		Trust	Exploitation
Player 1	Trust	a, a	$-b, a + x$
	Exploitation	$a + x, -b$	$0, 0$

Figure 2.7 Barter exchange ($0 < b < a, 0 < x$).

met with "double defection." Furthermore, defection is also "the opposite of trust" (Barney and Hansen, 1994, p. 176). Therefore, it can be assumed that in the matching process of the barter economy, each individual has two actions, namely trust or exploit (i.e., defection), which can be characterized as shown in the interdependent structure illustrated in Figure 2.7.

In Figure 2.7, the columns and rows represent players who have two bartering choices, namely trust or exploit. As the matrix indicates, mutual trust provides the payoff a for both players and mutual exploitation earns nothing. However, one player selecting trust and the other exploitation leads them to obtain $(-b)$ or $(a + x)$. This model is equal to the PD game that captures an important two-sided variant characteristic: two participants are determined to exploit interdependently in a symmetric matching process of bartering under uncertainties. Because unilateral exploitation surpasses single trust ($(a + x) > a$ and $0 > (-b)$) under uncertainties and thereby is unbeaten, the two bartering individuals rationally persist with unilateral exploitation throughout their interactions irrespective of the opponent's choice. Meanwhile, the dilemma is also evident in the barter economy: each side attempts to exploit the other, resulting in lower payoffs for both than those under mutual trust ($0 < a$). Overall, this design reflects the basic feature of bartering that a two-sided variant PD exists (both are willing to exploit) because of the presence of a symmetric structure with "double opportunism."

Barter economy

In order to explore trust phenomena in a barter economy with respect to the system of trust, I next concentrate on defining the barter economy. First, the components of the system of trust including its elements, interdependence, micro-to-macro transitions, and so on are elaborated on. The organizational function of exchange systems on the system of trust is focused upon by stressing the emergence of an exchange structure. With this consideration, I refer to barter exchange and design it as a symmetric structure – two-sided variant PD across homogeneous matches. Hence, I define the barter economy as follows:

> In a large interaction, individuals with different behavioral patterns, such as trust or exploit actions, are symmetrically matched in that they interdependently act. Nevertheless, once matched, they are constrained by different forms of interdependence (e.g., behavioral and evolutionary interdependences) when making decisions. The system of trust is a subsystem of bartering that is affected by interactive bartering over time through the outcomes of decisions.

Money and trust

In the last part of the discussion, individual trust in the barter economy is assumed to be constrained by how individuals interact over time. In this way, trust is presumed to be linked to the interdependence structure created by the barter economy. Following this point, the original extension of the link between money and trust was by Simmel (1990), who argued that interdependence is the starting point of all phenomena in society and that monetary exchange is an important process that binds individuals and trust. Skaggs (1998) also supported this statement by pointing to the emergence of trust because of the intervention of money. He stated that the emergence of money in exchange may link a series of credits at either the individual or the organizational level, where "individuals possessing financial wealth were willing to entrust their money to those in need of liquid funds in exchange for promises to repay the loan principle plus interest in the future" (p. 453). This generates a network of credit that implicitly supports trust in a society.

After being influenced by Simmel's theory of money and trust, Coleman (1990) presented a simple monetary exchange process (see Figure 2.8), arguing that "money enables two parties to break apart the two halves of the double coincidence of a barter transaction" (p. 120). As shown in the discussion on barter exchange, credit issues emerge because of the lack of money, while the money that arises must transfer this credit to institutions, facilitating the exchange (once again, the example of the one-to-many relationships created in bartering is relevant here). Individual *A* needs the goods of *B*, but individual *B* surely exchanges with *C*. In this case, *A* gives fiat money to *B* in return for the goods on the condition that *B* believes that the

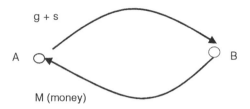

Figure 2.8 Monetary exchange (Coleman, 1990).

fiat money will be accepted by *C*, as the government had promised that it could be utilized in each transaction. By considering the influence of money on trust, Coleman (1990) took trust to be a linear system in asymmetric exchange that is influenced by price. However, despite its achievements, Coleman's linear system somewhat neglects the fact that trust is a dynamic outcome of interdependence in nature.

Money matches: Asymmetric structure – one-sided variant PD across heterogeneous matches

As in Simmel (1990), Coleman (1990), and Skaggs (1998), I regard the monetary economy as an interactive one and model money as the medium of exchange, which creates two roles in asymmetric exchange (i.e., buyer and seller). As mentioned above, barter exchange is characterized by the goods-for-goods model, while monetary exchange has a money-to-goods structure. In monetary exchange, individuals that have money want to exchange with those that own goods. I define individuals with money as buyers and those with goods as sellers (as in the microeconomics relationship of producers and consumers). Each monetary exchange thus involves two people from differential populations (i.e., it has an asymmetric structure).

As recognized, one-sided defection by sellers emerges when they pursue self-interests. To explain this interdependent structure in a monetary economy, I employ the one-sided variant PD game (also called as the trust-honor game; James, 2002) (see Figure 2.9) compared with the two-sided variant PD game in the barter economy. In this model, there is an asymmetric context between a buyer and a seller. The buyer has two choices: trust and distrust (deciding not to trade), while the seller chooses between honor and exploit actions. The incentive of the seller, as noted in monetary exchange, is to exploit the trust of the buyer, while the buyer has to gamble as to whether to trust the seller. For example, for the seller, choosing exploitation takes advantage of the selection of honor $((a + x) > a)$, irrespective of the choice

Seller

		Honor	Exploitation
Buyer	Trust	a, a	–b, a + x
	Distrust	0, – f	0, 0

Figure 2.9 Monetary exchange $(0 < f < b < a < a + x, 0 < x)$.

Note: f is a cost for the honor by seller when buyer chooses the distrust, e.g. time cost.

of the buyer under uncertainties (i.e., unilateral exploitation), whereas the buyer has no strong incentive to behave either way.

James (2002) applied RCT to this model in order to analyze the emergence of trust between any two agents in exchange. Among the minority of economic and social scholars who apply this model to explain the trust problem in a specific way are Kreps (1990) and Miller (1974). In consideration of these authors, we employ this model as an interactive structure in monetary exchange that characterizes single defection by the seller in the exchange process because of the intervention of money.

Monetary economy

I model money as the medium of exchange that creates an asymmetric structure including two roles in the matching process. Then, it is assumed that this structure is a one-sided PD game by considering that sellers are willing to defect. Therefore, as defined in the barter economy, the monetary economy is defined as follows:

> In a large population, individuals have two roles (buyers and sellers) and they are asymmetrically matched. Sellers tend to exploit interdependently, while buyers decide whether to place trust. Nevertheless, once matched, they are constrained by different forms of interdependence (e.g., behavioral evolutionary interdependences) when making decisions. The system of trust is a subsystem of monetary exchange that is affected by interactive monetary exchange over time.

There is one issue left for readers. Money is also an institution involved in trust. However, this kind of trust is not our focus because it is an institutional trust rather than a generalized trust. While the former is enforced by the government, the latter is created by interactive processes in a population, as this research explores.

Internet and trust

Since the primitive exchanges on the Internet, the problem of trust has long received attention. Much has been studied about the trust crisis online, with researchers showing that it is still far from "achieving its potential as an e-marketplace due to consumer reluctance to engage in spontaneous transactions online" (Salam *et al.*, 2005, p. 73). Some scholars have even indicated that the failure of e-commerce is chiefly due to the lack of trust (Luo, 2002).

To address this question directly, I follow the previous elaborations of non-monetary (barter) and monetary exchanges by arguing that the emergence of an exchange structure on the Internet has strongly influenced trust, triggering this phenomenon when individuals are placed in large anonymous online interactions. This approach contrasts with those of previous studies that have considered trust to have a static causal relationship, influenced by certain factors, overlooking the fact that Internet exchange is dynamic (i.e., people vary their behaviors to pursue self-interest).

Indeed, the outcome of spontaneous exchange is undesirable when defection is considered. In monetary exchange, the problem of trust emerges because of exploitation by sellers. In terms of Internet exchange, this characteristic remains, and it is as fierce as ever.

Let us start by looking at the stock market. When assets are divided into stocks and exchanged on the Internet, irregular behaviors by listed companies usually arise (e.g., falsifying accounts, operating insider dealing, spreading false news), thereby reducing investor confidence and thus trust in interactions. Similarly, on online platforms such as eBay, consumers often fear that sellers may provide fake or low-quality goods, or even nothing, after they have paid. For example, Gregg and Scott (2008), in their analysis of eBay profiles made up of comments from buyers and sellers, found that opportunistic behavior by sellers strongly affects the decision to trust. For example, 36 percent of complaints in 2003 were related to the comment "item paid but not received," and this increased to 39 percent by 2005.

Thus, one-sided defection by sellers, created by asymmetric information, is a characteristic of Internet exchange. However, another feature is adding enforcement mechanisms into exchange procedures to prevent this behavior.

When deciding whom to trust, reputation is considered if reputation effects exist. For example, by tracing the history of Maghribi traders in medieval trade, Greif (1989) found that reputation effects played an important role in surmounting cheating, especially when coalitions were small and information floating. Moreover, Milgrom *et al.* (1990) and Gambetta (1993) stated that when reputation effects are enforced by third parties such as coalitions and associations, trade is promoted despite abnormal behavior by merchants. Kandori (1992), similar to Ellison (1994), argued that word-of-mouth as a reputation mechanism can sanction fraud when a community is small. Hence, reputation effects are suggested to escape from the trust predicament and help penalize defection.

Online platforms such as Amazon and eBay that organize social coopertion are cases in point (Güth and Kliemt, 2004), showing that embedding enforcements allows reputation effects to work. Much has been written about the relationship between enforcements and trust by studying the reputation system on eBay. For example, Kalyanam and McIntyre (2001) showed that the evaluation score on eBay can have a positive effect on the trading volumes of sellers: when the scores of sellers are higher than average, more cooperation flourishes. Similarly, Livingston (2005) concluded that a higher reputation can lead to a good price in the final auction.

In addition to B2B transactions such as those on Amazon and eBay, C2C exchange (e.g., Alibaba) can also design a series of enforcements such as "real-name registration." Without enforcements on online platforms, people would never trust anyone in a *very large anonymous exchange arena*. However, when interactions occur on a meso-sized platform (network), even without the presence of enforcements, people self-organize to trust one another. For more details, refer to Elsner and Heinrich (2009).

The discussion presented here confirms that reputation effects kept by enforcements can maintain trust on the Internet. However, when combining one-sided defection with reputation effects, the question of how these characteristics of Internet exchange influence trust in large interactions, when considered in an interdependence structure, arises.

Internet matches: Asymmetric structure with enforcements –
across heterogeneous matches

The above discussion is linked to trust by considering one-sided defection and reputation effects on the Internet. Compared with the exchange structure in the monetary economy, it continues to be asymmetric, but it provides a reputation mechanism in each transaction that aims to punish poor behavior. Thus, an exchange structure emerges, as defined in Figure 2.10.

Figure 2.10 indicates that the emergence structure of the Internet is characterized by adding the punishment effect m created by enforcements to the payoffs for exploitation. The emergence of such an interdependent structure presents two features: (i) the seller attempts to defect as in monetary exchange but is restricted because of the reputation mechanism and

Seller

	Honor	Exploitation
Buyer **Trust**	a, a	–b, a + x –m
Distrust	0, –f	0, 0

Figure 2.10 Internet exchange $(0 < f < b < a < a + x, 0 < x, m)$.

(ii) the exogenous parameter m may alter the incentive of the seller when it changes, thereby affecting trust phenomena (e.g., evolution and stability). I present these treatments in Chapter 5.

Some readers may puzzle over the question of why Internet exchange has enforcement effects when monetary exchange does not. Put simply, enforcements in monetary exchange are not embedded into exchange procedures but rather only work when defection has occurred. This effect in monetary exchange can be treated as enforcement afterward, which is seen as noise in trust dynamics, as explored in Chapter 6.

Internet economy

As previously, we define the Internet economy as follows:

> In a large interaction, individuals have two roles (buyers and sellers) and they are asymmetrically matched on the Internet. Sellers have the choice to defect, while buyers decide whether to place trust. Nevertheless, once matched, they are constrained by different forms of interdependence (i.e., behavioral and evolutionary interdependences) when making decisions. Sellers are concerned about their reputations when reputation effects exist on the Internet. The system of trust is a subsystem of exchange that is affected by interactive Internet exchange over time.

Summary

The purpose of this chapter was to provide a theoretical foundation for the analysis of emergent trust. As noted in this chapter, the theory of the system of trust initiated by Coleman (1982) is referred to because previous economic theories rarely recognized the influence of the interactive context on trust. This theory is transferred to the economic context of exchange by combining agents, behaviors, interdependences, and micro-to-macro and macro-to-micro transitions into a framework that centers on direct interdependence and its structures. By using this framework, it was found that the emergence of structures in exchange systems (i.e., barter, monetary, Internet) is related to the emergence of trust. The presented analysis defined these exchanges as (i) a symmetric structure – a two-sided PD across homogeneous matches in barter exchange; (ii) an asymmetric structure – a one-sided PD across heterogeneous matches in monetary exchange; and (iii) an asymmetric structure with enforcements in Internet exchange.

With these foundations, we can next develop a co-evolving theory of exchange systems and trust by describing and analyzing the interactive trust phenomena (e.g., evolution and stability) placed on different exchange structures brought about by different exchange contexts. This approach is described in Figure 2.11.

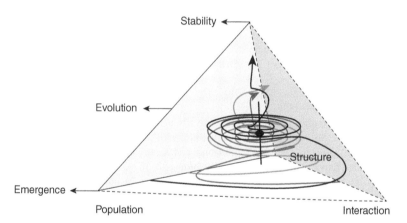

Figure 2.11(a) Longitudinal structure.

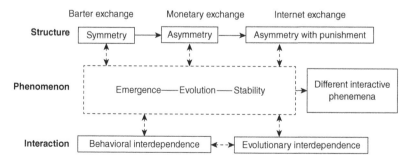

Figure 2.11(b) Horizontal structure.

The remainder of this study analyzes the emergence, evolution, and stability of trust by using the evolutionary approach discussed in Chapter 3 in order to complete the development of this theory. Note that in the analyses presented throughout the rest of the book, I assume that dynamic interactions are not affected by noise (e.g., structured interactions, impact of institutions) in micro-to-macro and macro-to-micro transitions. This point is addressed in Chapter 6, where the impact of noise is considered in general and specific noise, namely structured interactions, assessed in particular to explain the varieties of changes of trust.

References

Akerlof, G.A. 1970. The Market for "Lemons": Quality Uncertainty and the Market Mechanism. *Quarterly Journal of Economics*, 84(3), 488–500.

Arrow, K.J. 1970. *Essays in the Theory of Risk-Bearing*. Chicago, IL: Chicago University Press.

Arrow, K.J. 1973. *Information and Economic Behavior*. Stockholm: Federation of Swedish Industries.

Arrow, K.J. 1985. The Economics of Agency. In: Pratt, J., Zeckhauser, R. (Eds), *Principals and Agents: The Structure of Business*. Boston, MA: Harvard Business School Press, 37–51.

Axelrod, R., Hamilton, W.D. 1981. The Evolution of Cooperation. Science, 211(4489), 1390–1396.

Barney, J.B., Hansen, M.H. 1994. Trustworthiness as a Source of Competitive Advantage. *Strategic Management Journal*, 15(8), 175–190.

Barrear, D., Buskens, V. 2007. Imitation and Learning Under Uncertainty: A Vignette Experiment. *International Sociology*, 22, 367–396.

Bigley, G.A., Pearce, J.L. 1998. Straining for Shared Meaning in Organization Science: Problems of Trust and Distrust. *Academy of Management Review*, 23(3), 405–421.

Bradach, J., Eccles, R.G. 1989. Price, Authority and Trust: From Ideal Types to Plural Forms. *Annual Review of Sociology*, 15, 97–118.

Coleman, J.S. 1982. Systems of Trust: A Rough Theoretical Framework. *Angewandte Sozial-forschung*, 10(3), 277–299.

Coleman, J.S. 1990. *Foundations of Social Theory*. Cambridge, MA: Harvard University Press.

Cummings, L.L., Bromiley, P. 1996. The Organizational Trust Inventory (OTI): Development and Validation. In: Kramer, R.M., Tyler, T.R. (Eds), *Trust in Organizations*. Thousand Oaks, CA: Sage, 302–330.

Dopfer, K. 1986. The Histonomic Approach to Economics: Beyond Pure Theory and Pure Experience. *Journal of Economic Issues*, 20(4), 989–1010.

Dyer, J. 2000. The Determinants of Trust in Supplier–Buyer Relations in the U.S., Japan, and Korea. *Journal of International Business Studies*, 31, 259–285.

Edgeworth, F.Y. 1881. *Mathematical Psychics*. London: Kegan Paul.

Eisenhardt, K.M. 1989. Agency Theory: An Assessment and Review. *Academy of Management Review*, 14(1), 57–74.

Ellison, G. 1994. Cooperation in the Prisoner's Dilemma with Anonymous Random Matching. *Review of Economic Studies*, 61(3), 567–588.

Elsner, W. 2013. *Microeconomics of Interactive Economies: Evolutionary, Institutional, and Complexity Perspectives*. Cheltenham, Northampton, MA: Edward Elgar Publishing Limited.

Elsner, W., Heinrich, T. 2009. A Simple Theory of "Meso": On the Co-evolution of Institutions and Platform Size – With an Application to Varieties of Capitalism and "Medium-sized" Countries. *Journal of Socio-Economics*, 38(5), 843–858.

Elsner, W., Schwardt, H. 2014. Trust and Arena Size: Expectations, Institutions, and General Trust, and Critical Population and Group Sizes. *Journal of Institutional Economics*, 10(1), 107–134.

Engineer, M. 2001. Bargains, Barter, and Money. *Review of Economic Dynamics*, 4, 188–209.

Friedman, J.W. 1977. *Oligopoly and the Theory of Games*. Amsterdam: North Holland.

Fudenberg, D., Imhof, L.A. 2008. Monotone Imitation Dynamics in Large Populations. *Journal of Economic Theory*, 140, 229–245.

Gambetta, D. 1988. Can We Trust in Trust? In: Gambetta, D. (Ed.), *Trust: Making and Breaking Cooperative Relations*. New York, NY: University of Oxford, 213–237.

Gambetta, D. 1993. *The Sicilian Mafia: The Business of Protection*. Cambridge, MA: Harvard University Press.

Gaunersdorfer, A., Hofbauer, J., Sigmund, K. 1991. On the Dynamics of Asymmetric Games. *Theoretical Population Biology*, 39, 345–357.

Gregg, D., Scott, J.E. 2008. A Typology of Complaints about eBay Sellers. *Communication of the ACM*, 51(4), 69–74.

Greif, A. 1989. Reputation and Coalitions in Medieval Trade: Evidence on the Maghribi Traders. *Journal of Economic History*, 49(4), 857–881.

Gulati, R. 1995. Does Familiarity Breed Trust? The Implications of Repeated Ties for Contractual Choice in Alliances. *Academy of Management Journal*, 38, 85–112.

Güth, W., Kliemt, H. 2004. The Evolution of Trust (Worthiness) in the Net. *Analyse & Kritik*, 26, 203–219.

Hardin, R. 2006. *Trust: Key Concepts*. Cambridge, UK: Polity Press.

Hirshleifer, J. 1999. There are Many Evolutionary Pathways to Cooperation. *Journal of Bioecoomics*, 1(1), 73–93.

Hollis, M. 1998. *Trust within Reason*. Cambridge, UK: Cambridge University Press.

Hosmer, L.T. 1995. Trust: The Connecting Link between Organizational Theory and Philosophical Ethics. *Academy of Management Review*, 20(2), 379–403.

James, H.S. Jr. 2002. The Trust Paradox: A Survey of Economic Inquiries into the Nature of Trust and Trustworthiness. *Journal of Economic Behavior & Organization*, 47(3), 291–307.

Jensen, M., Meckling, W.H. 1976. Theory of the Firm: Managerial Behavior, Agency Costs and Ownership Structure. *Journal of Financial Economics*, 3(4), 305–360.

Johnson, S., Kaufmann, D., Shleifer, A. 1997. The Unofficial Economy in Transition. *Brookings Papers on Economic Activity*, 2, 159–239.

Kalyanam, K., McIntyre, S. 2001. Return on Reputation in Online Auction Markets. Working paper, Santa Clara University.

Kandori, M. 1992. Social Norms and Community Enforcement. *Review of Economic Studies*, 59, 63–80.

Kandori, M., Mailath, G.J., Rob, M.R. 1993. Learning, Mutation, and Long Run Equilibria in Games. *Econometrica*, 61, 29–56.

Kollock, P. 1994. The Emergence of Exchange Structures: An Experimental Study of Uncertainty, Commitment, and Trust. *American Journal of Sociology*, 100(2), 313–345.

Kreps, D. 1990. *A Course in Microeconomic Theory*. Princeton, NJ: Princeton University Press.

Kreps, D.M., Milgrom, P., Roberts, J., Wilson, R. 1982. Rational Cooperation in the Finitely Repeated Prisoners' Dilemma. *Journal of Economic Theory*, 27, 245–252.

Lane, C. 1998. Introduction: Theories and Issues in the Study of Trust. In: Lane, C., Bachmann, R. (Eds), *Trust Within and Between Organizations: Conceptual Issues and Empirical Applications*. Oxford: Oxford University Press, 1–30.

Livingston, J. 2005. How Valuable is a Good Reputation? A Sample Selection Model of Internet Auctions. *Review of Economics and Statistics*, 87(3), 453–465.

Luo, X. 2002. Trust Production and Privacy Concerns on the Internet: A Framework Based on Relationship Marketing and Social Exchange Theory. *Industrial Marketing Management*, 31(2), 111–118.

Maynard Smith, J. 1982. *Evolution and the Theory of Games*. Cambridge, UK: Cambridge University Press.

Milgrom, P., North, D.C., Weingast, B.R. 1990. The Role of Institutions in the Revival of Trade: The Law Merchant, Private Judges and the Champagne Fairs. *Economics and Politics*, 2(1), 1–23.

Miller, A.H. 1974. Political Issues and Trust in Government: 1960–1970. *American Political Science Review*, 68, 951–972.

Möllering, G. 2001. The Nature of Trust: From Georg Simmel to a Theory of Expectation, Interpretation and Suspension. *Sociology*, 35, 403–420.

Möllering, G. 2006. *Trust: Reason, Routine, Reflexivity*. Oxford: Elsevier.

Nooteboom, B. 1996. Trust, Opportunism and Governance: A Process and Control Model. *Organization Studies*, 17(6), 985–1010.

Nowak, M.A., Sasaki, A., Taylor, C., Fudenberg, D. 2004. Emergence of Cooperation and Evolutionary Stability in Finite Populations. *Nature*, 428, 646–650.

Orléans, A. 1998. The Ambivalent Role of Imitation in Decentralized Collective Learning. In: Lazaric, N., Orenz, E.H. (Eds), *Trust and Economic Learning*. Cheltenham, and Northampton, MA: Edward Elgar, 124–141.

O'Sullivan, A., Sheffrin, S.M. 2003. *Economics: Principles in Action*. Upper Saddle River, NJ: Pearson Prentice Hall.

Popper, K. 1945. *The Open Society and its Enemies*. Princeton, NJ: Princeton University Press.

Rose, D. 2011. *The Moral Foundation of Economic Behavior*. New York, NY: Oxford University Press.

Ross, S. 1973. The Economic Theory of Agency: The Principle's Problem. *American Economic Review*, 63(2), 134–139.

Rusbult, C.E., Van Lange, P.A.M. 2003. Interdependence, Interaction and Relationships. *Annual Review of Psychology*, 54, 351–375.

Salam, A.F., Lyer, L., Palvia, P., Singh, R. 2005. Trust in E-commerce. *Communications of The ACM*, 48(2), 73–77.

Selten, R. 1980. A Note on Evolutionary Stable Strategies in Asymmetric Contests. *Journal of Theoretical Biology*, 84, 93–101.

Shapiro, S.P. 1987. The Social Control of Impersonal Trust. *American Journal of Sociology*, 93(3), 623–658.

Simmel, G. 1990. *The Philosophy of Money*. 2nd edition. London: Routledge. Translated from the 1907 German edition by Tom Bottomore and David Frisby [Original ed. 1900].

Simon, H. 1957. *Administrative Behavior*. New York, NY: The Free Press.

Skaggs, N.T. 1998. Debt as the Basis of Currency: The Monetary Economic of Trust. *American Journal of Economics and Sociology*, 57(4), 453–467.

Smith, A. 1776. *An Inquiry into the Nature and Causes of the Wealth of Nations*. Oxford: Oxford University Press.

Tullock, G. 1985. Adam Smith and the Prisoner's Dilemma. *Quarterly Journal of Economics*, 100(402), supplement, 1073–1081.

Von Neumann J., Morgenstern, O. 1944. *Theory of Games and Economic Behavior*. Princeton, NJ: Princeton University Press.

Weibull, J.W. 1998. What Have we Learned from Evolutionary Game Theory So Far? Research Institute of Industrial Economics. Working Papers 487, Research Institute of Industrial Economics. Available at: http://ideas.repec.org/p/hhs/iuiwop/0487.html (accessed 30 May 2015).

Whitener, E.M., Brodt, S.E., Korsgaard, M.A., Werner, J.M. 1998. Managers as Initiators of Trust: An Exchange Relationship Framework for Understanding Managerial Trustworthy Behavior. *Academy of Management Review*, 23(3), 513–530.

Williamson, O.E. 1975. *Markets and Hierarchies*. New York, NY: Free Press.

Williamson, O.E. 1983. Credible Commitments: Using Hostages to Support Exchange. *American Economic Review*, 73(4), 519–540.

Williamson, O.E. 1985. *The Economic Institutions of Capitalism: Firms, Markets, Relational Contracting*. New York, NY: Free Press.

Williamson, O.E. 1993. Calculativeness, Trust, and Economic Organization. *Journal of Law and Economics*, 36, 453–486.

Williamson, O.E. 1996. *The Mechanisms of Governance*. New York, NY: Oxford University Press.

3 Methodology

Applications of the evolutionary approach to scientific research in such fields as economics, sociology, biology, and computer science have undergone, in Hodgson's (2004) view, an important transformation over the past 20 years. In comparison with the other sciences, however, the evolutionary approach has long been used to study economics. Indeed, this approach can be seen in the earlier works of Smith, Hume, and Meng De Weir (Hodgson, 2004) as well as in the later writing of Marshall, Malthus, Schumpeter, and Hayek (Weibull, 1998). These kinds of earlier works analyzed the transformation of social institutions under Marxist economics and the German Historical School (Hodgson, 2006) in addition to Veblen's institutional change theory (Hodgson, 2008). The use of the evolutionary approach was driven by studies of evolution in biology after 1960, such as the works of Taylor and Jonker (1978). Indeed, after Maynard Smith (1974) introduced game theory to biology, the approach gradually developed and diverse economic theories such as Schumpeter theory and self-organizing theory formed.

Although it has diverse applications, the approach is mainly utilized to analyze the population distribution of behaviors (i.e., strategies) over time, of which the emergence, evolution, and stability of behaviors are key analytical components (Weibull, 1998).

In this chapter, two fundamental aspects of the approach, namely its basic concepts and modeling process, are firstly explained. In the section "Basic concepts," the main concepts of the approach (i.e., evolutionary game theory (EGT), replicator dynamics, emergence) are explained by concentrating on the widely cited literature. These concepts also serve to provide a foundation for understanding evolutionary modeling in the following section. The analytical process introduced in section "Evolutionary modeling" provides an overview in order to clarify what it is, how it works, and why I apply the approach in this study. In the section "Analysis in this study", these main concepts and the analytical process mentioned above are used to formulate the overall analytical design.

Basic concepts

EGT

EGT has become a crucial method of the evolutionary approach (Hamilton, 1964; Maynard Smith and Price, 1973; Taylor and Jonker, 1978; Weibull, 1995; Young, 1998). It originally derived from evolutionary biology, where it was applied to study how multiple organisms interact when their behaviors are driven by one another, thereby allowing researchers to predict the equilibria and dynamic properties of this process. EGT converts game-theoretical structures into interactive ones to analyze evolving behaviors among economic agents (Weibull, 1995), and these structures, similar to game theory, involve strategies and payoffs characterized by a matrix (see Figure 3.1).

The matrix in Figure 3.1 has two strategies (i.e., cooperation and defection), which are played by individuals in an interactive process. When two individuals with the same strategy interact, both will receive payoff *a* when they cooperate and payoff *d* when they defect. By contrast, when individuals that have different strategies interact, the cooperator receives payoff *b* and the defector payoff *c*. This matrix supports the tendency for EGT to suppose that individuals with bounded rationality transfer payoffs, in terms of self-strategy, whereas those with "super rationality" as assumed in game theory select self-strategy through payoffs. This is clearly a difference between EGT and one-shot game theory.

Replicator dynamics in an infinite well-fixed population

According to Weibull (1998), "Replicator dynamics is an explicit model of a selection process in evolutionary game theory, specifying how population shares of different pure strategies in a game evolve over time" (p. 5). As shown in the concept of EGT, individuals in an interactive process accumulate

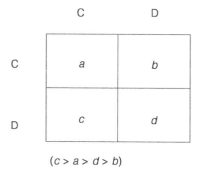

$(c > a > d > b)$

Figure 3.1 The "matrix of the game."

payoffs over time resulting from self-strategy, which emphasizes the need to recognize how behaviors with higher payoffs conflict with those with lower payoffs and to understand the prevalent outcomes. This is the aim of replicator dynamics, whose mathematical formulation comes from Taylor and Jonker (1978). In this model, a *population state*, a distribution about a pure strategy in a large population, is subject to "fitness." This is used to decide the rate of growth in a pure strategy after each episode of the evolutionary process (i.e., in each time step) and is mathematically equal to the value of the accumulated payoffs from all interactions minus the average payoff in the whole population at time t. It is written as follows:

$$f(i,s)_t = u(i,s)_t - u(s,s)_t,$$ (3.1)

where $u(i,s)_t$ is the payoff for an individual with strategy i at time t when he or she randomly encounters different strategies in the whole population and $u(i,s)_t$ is the average payoff for all types of strategies at time t.

When obtaining the fitness function, the population share of individuals undertaking strategy i in the whole population at time $(t+1)$ can be written as:

$$x_i(t+1) = x_i(t)\left[1 + f(i,s)_t\right],$$ (3.2)

where $x_i(t)$ is the population share of individuals with strategy i at time t.
Moreover, equation (3.2) can be mathematically treated as follows:

$$x_i(t+1) = x_i(t) + x_i(t) f(i,s)_t$$

$$\rightarrow \frac{x_i(t+1) - x_i(t)}{t+1-t} = x_i(t) f(i,s)_t$$

$$\rightarrow (\dot{x_i}) = x_i(t) f(i,s)_t.$$ (3.3)

In general, equations (3.2) and (3.3) are termed discrete and non-discrete models of replicator dynamics, respectively. In this study, non-discrete models of replicator dynamics are mainly applied. According to the basic assumptions of replicator dynamic models, the population is infinite and well-mixed: infinity means that the number of individuals grows without limitations in the long-term, while well-mixed illustrates that individuals are randomly matched in a large population at equal probabilities. However, in real-life societies, populations are usually finite in the short-term, with some individuals having high probabilities of meeting one person compared with another. Therefore, we consider imitation dynamic models (which are similar to replicator dynamic models) in the short-term, which suppose that the population is finite in structured interactions (Gintis, 2000; Nowak *et al.*, 2004; Santos *et al.*, 2006; Traulsen *et al.*, 2007).

Imitation dynamics in a finite structured population

As noted above, imitation dynamics often operate in finite structured populations and these are used to study the behaviors that evolve in the short-term. The explicit differences between replicator dynamic models (based upon infinite, well-fixed, long-run conditions) and imitation dynamic models (based upon finite, structured, short-term conditions) have been primary principles in the refined study of evolving behaviors in recent works. In this respect, imitation dynamics often provide more insight into collective activities, particularly in the short-term. For instance, when a financial crisis erupts, individuals imitate the behaviors of others at the door of the bank withdrawing their money, leading to bank runs. Similarly, when a restaurant is filled with customers, more and more people will want to eat there, supporting the special meaning and purpose of this research. In this sense, imitation dynamic models aim to describe a process in which people imitate one another, which subsequently drives changing behaviors. One rule of studies of imitation dynamics is that in every time step, one individual is randomly selected from the whole population to be compared with one of his or her neighbors. The probability of that person changing his or her behavior is proportional to the payoffs available. More details about imitation dynamic models are presented in Chapter 6, section "Trust in overlapping networks: Noise and varieties of change."

Emergence

In this study, the emergence of trust consists of two components: emergent trusting behavior and emergent trusting properties. The former comprises complex behaviors that arise through the interdependent actions of individuals in either one-shot or repeated interactions, whereas the latter are defined as a series of conditions for emergent trusting behavior, which are solutions to the dilemma of trust in exchange. For example, in PD games, the emergent phenomenon of complex behaviors may be cooperation if individuals participate in repeated interactions and if the discount factor δ is large enough (i.e., the folk theorem). Under such a circumstance, the discount factor δ and repeated setting are conceived as emergent properties for emergent cooperative behavior.

Evolution

In the literature, evolution is often referred to as all feasible manifestations of development and change in a broad class of system and a population of entities (Hodgson, 2006). In this study, the evolution of trust is explored in exchange systems (e.g., barter, monetary, Internet). The evolution of trust is a movement over time that describes a comprehensive evolutionary process driven by individuals interdependently interacting in a large population in different exchange systems. To present this movement, replicator and imitation dynamic models are applied in Chapters 5 and 6.

Stability

One of the key concepts of EGT for defining the stability of evolving behaviors is an evolutionarily stable strategy (ESS) (Maynard Smith and Price, 1973; Maynard Smith, 1982; Weibull, 1998). An ESS assumes that in a single population, all individuals initially use the same strategy x, but they cannot be invaded by an emerging small subpopulation of individuals who employ a distinct strategy y (Cressman, 1992). In this sense, this concept can be defined mathematically as follows. Suppose that in a large population in which in each time step every individual plays a symmetric game with an individual who is randomly selected from the whole population, there exist ϵ frequencies of mutant strategy $y \in \Delta$ and $(1 - \epsilon)$ individuals with the strategy $x \in \Delta$ exist ($\epsilon \in (0, 1)$). Let $g = \epsilon y + (1 - \epsilon)x$ be the population composition, which illustrates that there are ϵ frequencies of y and $(1 - \epsilon)$ frequencies of x. $E(x, g)$ and $E(y, g)$, respectively, are functions that represent the actual payoffs of an individual who plays strategies x and y when encountered with g. The formal concept of the evolutionary stability of a strategy can be defined as follows (Weibull, 1995, p. 36):

$x \in \Delta$ is an ESS if for every strategy $y \neq x$ there exists some $\bar{\epsilon}_y \in (0,1)$ such that inequality 3.4 holds for all $\epsilon \in (0, \bar{\epsilon}_y)$,

$$E\left[x, \epsilon y + (1 - \epsilon)x\right] > E\left[y, \epsilon y + (1-\epsilon)x\right]. \tag{3.4}$$

The stability of behaviors in evolution processes is defined in Chapter 5, section "Stability of trust." At this point, the definition provided offers a basic introduction to evolutionary stability, referring implicitly to the setting including populations, games, and strategies.

Evolutionary modeling

This section introduces the normal procedures of evolutionary modeling applied in the subsequent analysis presented in this thesis. In section "Basic concepts," I described the general concepts of evolutionary analysis. In this section, first the analytical process is illustrated, including the interactive structure, selection of evolutionary dynamics, calculation of the fitness function, and stability analysis. Then, together with each element, simple explanations are provided to help link the subsequent analysis.

Analytical process

Interactive structure

The section "Basic concepts" introduced the basic idea of EGT, namely that the payoffs of multiple organisms involved in a large population come from self-strategies on which they insist when they match in interactions. An important issue here is to define an interactive structure that involves the payoffs and strategies that characterize the basic matching type for interactions in order to reflect on the social structure at the micro level.

Discussion here is mainly based on the methodologies applied by Maynard Smith (1974, 1982), Cressman (1992), and Weibull (1995). The first step in the analysis of interactive structures is to define the strategies that exist in a population according to the empirical or theoretical reflections on a certain problem structure. To predict a collective outcome in this problem structure, these strategies are placed into an interactive process, which is labeled $\{s_1, s_2, s_3, ..., s_n\}$ and fixed over the lifetime. Meanwhile, in this process, the different interacting strategies produce a series of payoffs, which are assumed to be $\{\pi_1, \pi_2, \pi_3, ..., \pi_n\}$. Thus, an interactive structure can be written as:

$$
\begin{array}{c}
S_1 \quad S_2 \ ... \ S_n \\[6pt]
\begin{array}{c} S_1 \\ S_2 \\ \vdots \\ S_n \end{array}
\begin{pmatrix}
\pi_1 & \cdots & \pi_n \\
\vdots & \ddots & \vdots \\
\pi_n & \cdots & \pi_n
\end{pmatrix}
\end{array}
$$

The strategies and problem structures embedded in different exchange systems were defined in Chapter 2. For example, the barter system has two strategies, namely trust and exploit, with a two-sided variant feature characterized by a PD game.

Although these are presented as a game-theoretical model, based on the description above, these models can be changed into interactive structures by insisting that strategies are seen as individuals in a matching process in a population that is fixed over the lifetime of individuals. For example, in the barter system, an interactive structure can be presented as shown in Figure 3.2 (compare with Figure 2.7).

Selection of evolutionary dynamic models

Having introduced the two basic types of evolutionary dynamic models (i.e., replicator and imitation dynamic models), the important principle for selecting them is based on whether the interaction is structured. If individuals

	Trust	Exploit
Trust	a	$-b$
Exploit	$a + x$	0

Figure 3.2 The interactive structure in the barter economy.

randomly interact, replicator dynamic models are used; if they structurally interact (e.g., in network interactions), imitation dynamic models are used.

In this study, replicator dynamic models are discussed in Chapter 5 by focusing on the long-term evolutionary process of trust in interactive barter, monetary, and Internet exchanges without structured interactions. More detail about replicator dynamic models including their concepts and procedures can also be found in this chapter. However, these are partly reconsidered by introducing imitation dynamic models in Chapter 6. This chapter aims to explain why trust varies over time and argues that it results from structured interactions in overlapping networks.

Calculating the fitness function

The fitness function is a payoff-dependent form because of strategic interactions. A core idea in biology is to describe how strong genes reproduce (Moran, 1962). In economics, this sense of reproduction is defined as the growth rate of a certain strategy after each generation of the evolutionary process. As suggested above, while each individual is fixed to a certain strategy, he or she will accumulate payoffs over interactions. It makes sense that when a type of strategy can achieve a higher-than-average payoff across the whole population over time, it naturally is assumed to increase rapidly compared with the other parts of the population. To express this basic idea, the calculation of the fitness function largely varies in response to the selection of evolutionary dynamic models. To calculate the fitness function in imitation dynamic models, see Chapter 6, section "Trust in overlapping networks: Noise and varieties of change." Here, I focus on the fitness function in replicator dynamic models, with reference to equation (3.1).

Let me provide a simple example of how equation (3.1) is calculated in replicator dynamic models. For simplicity, it is assumed that a traffic conflict emerges because two kinds of individuals drive their cars in random pairwise interactions. People follow one of two strategies when they encounter, namely turning right or left. It is also assumed that at the beginning, there exist x individuals that turn left and $(1 - x)$ that turn right. When they interact, two possible outcomes arise:

- When an individual turning left meets one turning right, they crash.
- When two identical strategies interact, they coordinate successfully.

Hence, the interactive structure can be written as follows:

$$
\begin{array}{c}
\quad\ L\ \ R \\
\begin{array}{c} L \\ R \end{array}
\begin{pmatrix} 8 & 0 \\ 0 & 8 \end{pmatrix}.
\end{array}
$$

Let π^{left} be the expected payoff of an individual turning left at time t and π^{right} that for an individual turning right. Suppose $\pi(m\backslash n)$ indicates the payoff for strategy m when it encounters strategy n. The calculation of the fitness function is shown as follows (for more information, see section "Basic concepts"):

The expected payoff for an individual turning left at time t is:

$$\pi^{left} = x\pi(left \backslash left) + (1-x)\pi(left \backslash right) = x8 + (1-x)0 = 8x.$$

The expected payoff for an individual turning right at time t is:

$$\pi^{right} = x\pi(right \backslash left) + (1-x)\pi(right \backslash right) = x0 + (1-x)8 = 8(1-x).$$

The average payoff over the whole population at time t is calculated as:

$$\pi^{average} = x\pi^{left} + (1-x)\pi^{right} = 8x^2 + 8(1-x)^2.$$

Hence, the fitness function of individuals turning left is:

$$f^{left} = \pi^{left} - \pi^{average} = 8x - 8x^2 - 8(1-x)^2 = 8 - 8x.$$

Stability analysis

After selecting evolutionary dynamic models and calculating the fitness function, thus presenting a dynamic process for a certain strategy over time, it is necessary for us to know where the process is stable by using stability analysis (Maynard Smith and Price, 1973). A key concept in the evolutionary approach is ESS, which has been widely utilized in the literature to display the strength of a strategy when a few intruders appear in a population. After that, the development of stability analysis follows three directions: (i) confining stability analysis to symmetric interactions within a single population (Weibull, 1995); (ii) focusing on asymmetric interactions within heterogeneous populations (Selten, 1980); and (iii) extending the static prediction to a dynamic one (Maynard Smith, 1982). Therefore, the application of stability analysis is contingent on circumstances such as whether the population is single or multiple.

Having specified the main analytical process to perform an evolutionary approach and introduced several concepts to understand the general components, I next describe the subsequent analysis presented in this study.

Analysis in this study

Trust emergence in Chapter 4

Chapter 4 applies two approaches based on the theory described in this chapter, namely that trust is rational and that it is affected by two forms of interdependence (i.e., behavioral and evolutionary interdependences) in a system of trust. In behavioral interdependence, the emergence of trusting behavior seems to directly encapsulate the partner's actions rather than taking them for granted, as occurs in a one-shot situation. In this situation, both matching individuals need to use rational methods of trust (e.g., expectation, reason, etc.) to place trust (see Chapter 2, section "The concept of trust in economic exchange") in order to reduce uncertainty. These methods can be analyzed by using game theory, specifically by considering the incentives and rationality in the exchange structure. Through game theory, this study proposes the sufficient conditions for emergent trust behavior in exchange. In evolutionary interdependence, individuals are affected not only by behaviors in a single interaction but also directly or indirectly by the outward behaviors that exist in dynamic processes. To model this dynamic impact on the emergence of trust, the imitation dynamic model from the evolutionary approach is used. Throughout this analysis, these methods serve as an answer for the paradox of trust, namely how people can constrain self-interests in order to trust.

Trust evolution and stability analysis in Chapter 5

Chapter 5 pays attention to how trust evolves and stabilizes over time and examines the different phenomena in exchange systems. This is carried out by using the evolutionary approach in two steps. First, taking the micro–macro transition of trust in the system of trust as a replicator dynamic process provided the population is infinite and well-mixed, focuses on the impact of the emergence of interactive structures from exchange systems on the evolution of trust. These replicator dynamic models depend on interactive structures, characterized by symmetric and asymmetric replicator dynamic models, which cater for the characteristics of interactive structures discussed in Chapter 2, section "Trust in the evolution of exhange systems: Interdependence structures and populations in the system of trust." Second, evolutionary analysis suggests a need for stability analysis that finds where this transition in the system of trust is stable. This stability analysis is organized into two stages. First, a static prediction approach is applied, which aims to confirm the stability of behaviors by comparing the payoffs defined in stability concepts. These stability concepts include the ESS used in the literature in the symmetric context as well as those developed in this study for the asymmetric context. Second, a dynamic prediction approach is used to reconsider the replicator dynamic models utilized and find how these dynamic processes are stable and where the stable points are with respect to an exchange setting that is supposed to be dynamic. The core of this approach is the concept of SS.

Trust varieties analysis in Chapter 6

Chapter 6 highlights the impact of noises on the evolution of trust, resulting in varieties of changes in trust. Based on the theory of Foster and Young (1990), the analysis first takes whole noises as a single noise in a single random process. Then, this single noise is re-entered into the replicator dynamic models presented in Chapter 5 to focus on the strength of the noise. The analysis is based on imitation dynamic models in an overlapping network model by emphasizing the influence of structured interactions, which create a specific noise in real interactions and provide a specific reason for the varieties of changes in trust. The imitation dynamic model is based on the works of Gintis (2000) and Santos *et al.* (2006).

References

Cressman, R. 1992. *The Stability Concept of Evolutionary Game Theory: A Dynamic Approach.* Berlin: Springer-Verlag.

Foster, D., Young, P. 1990. Stochastic Evolutionary Game Dynamics. *Theoretical Population Biology*, 38(2), 219–232.

Gintis, H. 2000. *Game Theory Evolving.* Princeton, NJ: Princeton University Press.

Hamilton, W.D. 1964. The Genetical Evolution of Social Behavior, I, II. *Journal of Theoretical Biology*, 7, 1–16, 17–52.

Hodgson, G.M. 2004. *The Evolution of Institutional Economics: Agency, Structure and Darwinism in American Institutionalism.* London and New York, NY: Routledge.

Hodgson, G.M. 2006. *Economics in the Shadows of Darwin and Marx: Essays on Institutional and Evolutionary Themes*. Cheltenham: Edward Elgar.

Hodgson, G.M. 2008. Prospects for Economic Sociology. *Philosophy of the Social Sciences*, 38(1), 133–149.

Maynard Smith, J. 1974. The Theory of Games and Evolution of Animal Conflicts. *Journal of Theoretical Biology*, 47, 209–221.

Maynard Smith, J. 1982. *Evolution and the Theory of Games*. Cambridge, UK: Cambridge University Press.

Maynard Smith, J., Price, G.R. 1973. The Logic of Animal Conflict. *Nature*, 246, 15–18.

Moran, P.A.P. 1962. *The Statistical Processes of Evolutionary Theory*. Oxford: Clarendon Press.

Nowak, M.A., Sasaki, A., Taylor, C., Fudenberg, D. 2004. Emergence of Cooperation and Evolutionary Stability in Finite Populations. *Nature*, 428, 646–650.

Santos, F.C., Pacheco, J.M., Lenaerts, T. 2006. Evolutionary Dynamics of Social Dilemmas in Structured Heterogeneous Populations. *PNAS*, 103(9), 3490–3494.

Selten, R. 1980. A Note on Evolutionary Stable Strategies in Asymmetric Contests. *Journal of Theoretical Biology*, 84, 93–101.

Taylor, P., Jonker, L. 1978. Evolutionary Stable Strategies and Game Dynamics. *Mathematical Biosciences*, 40, 145–156.

Traulsen, A., Pacheco, J.M., Nowak, M.A. 2007. Pairwise Comparison and Selection Temperature in Evolutionary Game Dynamics. *Journal of Theoretical Biology*, 246, 522–529.

Weibull, J.W. 1995. *Evolutionary Game Theory*. London: MIT Press.

Weibull, J.W. 1998. What Have we Learned from Evolutionary Game Theory So Far? Research Institute of Industrial Economics. Working Papers 487, Research Institute of Industrial Economics. Available at: http://ideas.repec.org/p/hhs/iuiwop/0487.html (accessed 30 May 2015).

Young, H.P. 1998. *Individual Strategy and Social Structure: An Evolutionary Theory of Institutions*. Princeton, NJ: Princeton University Press.

4 Emergence of trust

We cannot flourish without trust. This should be as plain to reason as it is to common sense. So reason should be able to show us what makes for a reliable social order, where people find it rational to trust one another.

(Hollis, 1998, p. 4)

Trust is rational and conditional (Hume, 1740; Smith, 1776; Granovetter, 1985; Gauthier, 1986; Binmore, 1993; Putnam, 1993; Hollis, 1998; Bruni and Sugden, 2000; Elsner and Schwardt, 2014). For example, according to Putnam (1993), "I trust you, because I trust her and she assures me that she trusts you" (p. 169). Moreover, "when we say we trust someone or that someone is trustworthy, we implicitly mean that the probability that he will perform an action that is beneficial or at least not detrimental to us is high enough for us to consider engaging in some form of cooperation with him" (Gambetta, 1988, p. 217). Indeed, "under appropriate conditions, trust can be recommended to rational persons" (Bruni and Sugden, 2000, p. 23).

In this chapter, the emergence of trust is supposed to be the unification of *rationality and the system of trust* in which individuals interdependently place trust. In this respect, it urges two settings for the emergence of trust due to interdependent forms – behavioral and evolutionary interdependences – at the micro level of this system (see Figures 2.5 and 2.12), given the rationality of agents. Therefore, this chapter follows the presented framework to explore the emergence of trust and to answer why self-seeking people temper their selfishness in order to trust.

To discuss the emergence of trust in behavioral interdependence, economists generally equate it with cooperation in a one-shot or repeated PD game (Deutsch, 1960; James, 2002; Hardin, 2006). Since trust emerges in "situations in which the risk one takes depends on the performance of another actor" (Coleman, 1990, p. 91), a PD game invents this situation (i.e., one person acting opportunistically is the poison of another co-operating). In this sense, studies have proposed a method for predicting the emergence of trust that is a consequence of rational actions. My study of behavioral interdependence builds on this recognition by defining the emergence of trust as risky trusting behavior for achieving exchange in interactive structures.

To discuss the emergence of trust in evolutionary interdependence, trust is placed based on imitation. To help us visualize this matter, a theoretical method from evolutionary biology is provided to extend the domain of research of trust in economics. By introducing the pairwise comparison process and Moran process, the emergence of trust is modeled as a dynamic outcome of individual behaviors – the incremental number of individuals that trust in a whole population – where individuals' behaviors are dynamically affected by imitating that comprises two processes.

By considering all these elements, the remainder of this chapter is structured as follows. The following section considers the emergence of trust in behavioral interdependence. To begin with, I review the literature on the application of behavioral interdependence on the emergence of trust, particularly referring to the works of Russell Hardin, Diego Gambetta, James Coleman, and Harvey S. James, to present how trust emerges through rational considerations (e.g., reason, expectation, and calculation) in behavioral interdependence. Then, the function of the mechanism design on the emergence of trust is explained, which emphasizes that exogenous environments should provide a foundation for behavioral interdependence to promote trust. In the section "Emergence of trust: Exogenous arrangements," the concept of imitating trust is first introduced, which serves to explain imitation dynamics. Then, I explain the method, involving the pairwise process and Moran process with a theoretical introduction and modeling illustrated in an example of trust in the barter system.

Trust in behavioral interdependence

The foundation of the emergence of trust in behavioral interdependence

Although there have been many attempts to understand and formalize why self-seeking people temper their selfishness in order to trust, research from an economic perspective is rare. Economic approaches suggest that incentives are important to explain the emergence of behaviors in economic interactions. A simple way to understand this is by regarding the statement "person A trusts person B" as an objective description that "A has an incentive to trust B." This statement corresponds to our basic hypothesis that individuals act interdependently. Hence, an individual tends not to trust his or her interaction partner in general, preferring to trust him or her condition-ally (i.e., following certain incentives). The analysis of incentives to trust in certain circumstances therefore aims to solve the emergence of trust issue.

In Chapter 2, I defined a number of core terms (e.g., expectation-based trust, reason-based trust, and calculation-based trust) to characterize a rational choice approach based on incentives to trust. In this section, these serve to model the emergence of trust in practice in order to indicate how individuals can trust, or how human rationality creates trust in the analysis of incentives. Here, two assumptions are necessary. First, individuals are assumed to act rationally in interactions, which means that each individual reasons in order to select the optimal outcome that provides the best response to his or her partner's selection in an interactive structure. Second, they are assumed to have common knowledge about the interactive structure, mean-ing that the conflicts embedded in interactive structures are known when both players decide who to trust. Although these assumptions are common in the literature, they serve as a foundation to use behavioral interdependence to examine the emergence of behavior in social science.

Expectation

Expectation is a common, rational action for humans when they are uncer-tain about something that may subsequently occur. Before cooperation, or even before meeting, we typically form an expectation that trusted individuals behave in a way that does not harm (Gambetta, 1988). Examples include investment pools, job markets (e.g., employers expect employees to have a certain ability), debit and credit, and so forth.

The function of expectation on evoking trust in economic studies is connected to probability, or probability estimation in the language of mathematics. A popular conceptualization of trust was pioneered by Coleman (1990), who characterized this function as follows: if the expected payoffs from trust are greater than the losses, individuals ration-ally place trust. Accordingly, we apply this idea to barter exchange to explain the trust paradox. The interdependent structure of barter exchange is shown in Figure 2.7.

According to the approach of Coleman (1990), the probability of *player 1* expecting *player 2* to select trust is p and to choose exploitation is $(1-p)$. Hence, the expected payoff for *player 1* to select trust is given by:

$$\pi_1^{Trust} = ap + b(1-p) = (a-b)p + b.$$

The expected payoff to choose exploitation is given by:

$$\pi_1^{Exploit} = (a+x)p + 0(1-p) = (a+x)p.$$

Thus, when $\pi_1^{Trust} > \pi_1^{Exploit}$ (i.e., $0 \le p < b/(x+b)$), *player 1* will rationally place trust in *player 2*. Similarly, the analysis is repeated for *player 2*. It follows that *player 2* will rationally trust *player 1* if $0 \le q < b/(x+b)$.

Despite the suggestion that trust has emerged here, I have exaggerated the function of expectation in this part because Coleman did not clearly explain how this subjective probability of individuals occurs (see also Möllering, 2006). In some sense, although unconsciously accepted, it is contingent on circumstances. For example, people often perceive whether the exchange partner is demonstrating trust based on signals before exchange starts. For example, awkward facial expressions might evoke thoughts about the trustworthiness of the partner, or after repeated exchange, trust through routine might evolve. Even though it is far more uncertain for us than for the individuals themselves, no further elaboration has been provided in the literature to help explain how individuals can trust in terms of expectation.

Reason

When discussing reason in decision-making, the following widespread doctrine is held: "I trust someone if I have reason to believe it will be in that person's interest to be trustworthy in the relevant way at the relevant time" (Hardin, 2006, p. 19). Trust, as encapsulated in Hardin's (2006) theory, first highlights the function of reason on trust. In Hardin's work, the formula for the emergence of trust is described as "individual *A* trust[s] *B* because of making a judgment with respect to *M*." For example, I trust you because you are my friend and you are valuable to me; hence, I encapsulate your interests in order to place trust.

In this context, strictly speaking, reason works only if the reason is clear for either of the two individuals and if the underlying payoffs are large when this behavior is performed. Nevertheless, in some cases individuals cannot avoid behavioral conflicts because of "reason," even if the criteria have been met. For example, they might engage in an interactive situation characterized by a zero-sum game. Under this circumstance, the rule of the game is simple: there can only be one winner. Reason encourages two people toward a conflict situation by considering this rule. In spite of these predicaments, however, reason can still be applied in many situations in which individuals place trust. Hardin (2006) outlined three clear and common reasons for individuals being routinely placed in a trust predicament: a recurring beneficial relationship, social embeddedness (e.g., with friends or relatives), and reputation.

First, a recurring beneficial relationship is sufficient reason to explain how trust emerges. If the alternative to receive benefits, relative to trust, is forgone, it suggests that some situations endow the trusting selection with higher payoffs. One such situation is the ongoing context. To some degree, this is implicitly recognized as a future value that can be created through partner relationships in long-run interactions, and thus it is a social, rational consideration among economic individuals. Under such a circumstance, agent *A* trusts *B* to cooperate because of the underlying benefits that arise from repeated cooperation in the future, and vice versa.

Suppose that *player 1* knows that *player 2* is likely to repeat an exchange, with $\delta(0 \leq \delta \leq 1)$ being a common discount factor that discounts future value. The interdependent structure is like the one presented in Figure 2.7. *1* encapsulates *2*'s interest to trust because the payoffs for choosing trust and exploitation, respectively, are given by:

$$\pi_1^{Trust} = a + a\delta + a\delta^2 + a\delta^3 + \cdots + a\delta^n = a / 1 - \delta,$$

$$\pi_1^{Exploit} = (a + x) + 0\delta + 0\delta^2 + \cdots + 0\delta^n = a + x.$$

This signifies that *player 1* trusts *player 2* because $\pi_1^{Trust} \geq \pi_1^{Exploit}$, namely $x / a + x < \delta \leq 1$. Similarly, the processes are suitable for *player 2*, too.

The analysis above shows that the high payoffs for selecting exploitation are compensated in a one-shot situation because of the outcome of the "shadow of the future" and so overlooked. Instead, the emergence of trust is taken for granted. With this conclusion in mind, we refocus on the common factor δ and assume that this is a static issue for every individual in exchange. Nevertheless, in reality it is fixed by chance and is typically more often dynamic in a market. It seems to be logical to regard trust as fragile if ongoing reasoning works in unstable "market" environments (because the future is uncertain). Hence, the stability of the market is important for the emergence of trust. It thus seems to be logical to think that when more people confide in the future, exchange flourishes because of the continual emergence of trust.

Of the other ways in which to view the emergence of trust, social embeddedness, roughly speaking, focuses on how economic agents decide on their present actions according to various ties (see Granovetter, 1985), while the other is reputation (see Greif, 1989).

Calculation

When the functions of expectation and reason are considered, they are to some degree based on the premise that people are capable of simply calculating. This discussion is not restricted to just a calculative sense but also expanded to a purposive sense. Trust is endowed with a purposive sense in terms of calculation partly because of the aim to reduce transaction costs.

By assuming that the exchange partner will act opportunistically, agents attempt to safeguard the exchange by using various institutionalized enforcements (e.g., executing the contract), if they perceive the partner to be trustworthy (Bigley and Pearce, 1998). However, imposing controls on opportunistic behavior should incur considerable costs, and thus reducing these by means of trust is rational. Indeed, Macaulay's (1963) statistical investigation found that companies stopped aiming for "complete" contracts as legal remedies were so costly and instead relied on trust when the trustworthiness of their partners could be perceived. However, TCT suggests that controls generate all sorts of costs (e.g., contracting costs), which leads to either costs c or possible punishment m in exchange. Then, conflicts could be altered by changing the payoffs (see Figure 4.1).

Figure 4.1 shows that enforcing a contract leads to two main changes to the payoff structure: on the one hand, cost c reduces the payoffs when the parties cooperate or when defection occurs; on the other hand, enforcements m on the action of single defection are imposed, which aim to reduce the payoffs for defection and improve trust. To consider the purposive sense of calculation for the emergence of trust, let us reconsider the function of expectation. It is common sense that even if enforcements are in place, the possibility to exploit remains. It is assumed that *player 2* with probability $p(0 \leq p \leq 1)$ selects trust and with $(1 - p)$ chooses exploit.

When *player 1* chooses trust or exploitation, the expected payoffs are given by:

$$\pi_1^{Trust} = (a-c)p + (-b-c)(1-p),$$

$$\pi_1^{Exploitation} = (a+x-m)p + (-c)(1-p).$$

If and only if $\pi_1^{Trust} > \pi_1^{Exploitation}$, namely $c < m - x - b / p$, player 1 will place trust in *player 2* under this enforcement. Based on this condition, it is clear that these costs should be kept at a certain level. When they become too

		Player 2	
		Trust	Exploitation
Player 1	Trust	$a - c, a - c$	$-b - c, a + x - m$
	Exploitation	$a + x - m, -b - c$	$-c, -c$

Figure 4.1 Barter exchange with enforcements ($0 < b \leq a < a + x$, $0 < c$, m).

high, and when the trustworthiness of the partner can be perceived, enforcement can be quite costly, possibly turning individuals toward trust, which is costless.

Emergence of trust: Exogenous arrangements

Real doubts exist in the long run about how exogenous arrangements can help these rational choice approaches of trust work in order to create trust. Would rational players, owing to certain institutional arrangements, prompt themselves to trust each other? This question complicates understanding the effect of *exogenous arrangements* on trust. In this section, I thus analyze, from an exogenous perspective, how trust emerges based on exogenous arrangements through which people expect, reason, or calculate.

Hirshleifer (1999) intended to distinguish the *payoff environment* and *game protocol* that are capable of triggering the emergence of behaviors. This logic allows us to explain how trust emerges by exogenously influencing them.

Chapter 2 proposed the interdependent structures presented in Figures 2.7, 2.9, and 2.10, namely barter, monetary, and Internet exchanges, to explore the emergence, evolution, and stability of trust. As emphasized here, these structures are identified as real exchange circumstances under which economic agents act interdependently and that result in different behaviors contingent on the different exchange circumstances (i.e., incentive structures). For example, in the barter economy, two-sided variant PD expresses that two sides have incentives to defect as the best response to the actions of the opposite side. In the literature, exchange environments are often called payoff environments because these conflicts are presented through payoff structures in mathematics. By contrast, the game protocol explains in a given exchange environment what kinds of strategies participants can follow and how they choose to move (i.e., the rules of the game). To broaden participants' outlooks, two treatments exist: when participants are assumed to take part in a one-shot interaction and when they join a repeated one. In the repeated context, the "shadow of the future" allows people to balance present and future payoffs, which may result in trust being placed, whereas defection prevails in a one-shot situation. In this section, I thus focus on the one-shot situation by considering moves and strategies that relate to the emergence of trust.

In a one-shot situation, people often confine their interests to the promise of the best response to partners' selections. This phenomenon, which induces them not to be concerned about their partners, mainly comes from the condition of "simultaneous moves," which makes actions unobservable for one or other party. Similarly, this suggests a special outcome for trust in certain exchange situations: in barter and monetary exchanges, people act opportunistically because defecting behavior is not insensitive to the part-ner's actions but rather leads to safe payoffs overall, the anticipated result of which is common defection (i.e., Pareto-inefficiency). For participants to be better off, from an academic perspective, the game protocol should aim to regulate this move before the beginning of the game by claiming a "sequential move." This simple treatment affects the behaviors in the interaction because first-mover behavior is observable.

Consider this condition in barter exchange (matrix 1 in Figure 2.7). It seems to be logical to deduce that if *player 1* chooses first, he or she will be concerned about the actions of *player 2*. Moreover, *player 2* could make a decision based on this action: if you choose trust, I choose trust or exploitation; if you choose exploitation, I choose exploitation. On the contrary, column 1 also shows that if exploitation is selected, nothing will be obtained, as row 1 definitely retaliates. Further, if trust is placed, he or she will receive payoff a or $(-b)$. According to the backward induction principle, if participants are rational, the first-mover player chooses exploitation because he or she knows the row player must choose exploitation to obtain a higher payoff $(a + x)$. Nevertheless, this analysis to some degree overlooks whether the first mover is also rational, who may tentatively trust in order to obtain a higher payoff a compared with nothing for selecting exploitation. Meanwhile, this trust is observable to the second mover, and he or she thus tends to cooperate (i.e., the TFT strategy in Axelrod, 1984). Accordingly, under such circumstances, the "sequential equilibrium" may not always be common exploitation; it may be common trust.

Monetary exchange (matrix 2 in Figure 2.9) can be more interesting than barter exchange. This pattern represents two heterogeneous people, namely a buyer as the column player and a seller as the row player, with the feature of one-sided defection. As stated in the previous section, this pattern is called one-sided variant PD, where the seller attempts to exploit the trust of the buyer. Under such a circumstance, if the "simultaneous move" is pre-arranged, the result of the game is (distrust, exploit) because the buyer knows that the seller will exploit this trust when it is placed, as the seller aims to get his or her payoff $(a + x)$. Consider the "sequential move" to be a special pre-arrangement. Hence, in contrast to before, this time the row player (i.e., the seller) is required to move first (when the column player moves first, the analysis and outcome are identical to those in barter exchange). If the seller wants to choose exploitation, the buyer must retali-ate and nothing is obtained. If he or she chooses honor, the payoff a or $(-b)$ is gained contingent on the choices of the buyer. However, it is much more possible that the buyer trusts, as choosing distrust leads to nothing for both parties. Therefore, the sequential equilibrium could be (trust, honor) when the row player moves first.

Based on who moves first in a given exchange environment, economic agents may form the trust necessary to overcome dilemma in exchange. Although there is reason to believe that these inferences are right, it is not enough to cover all types of "move" procedures or the decision-making processes of agents. These strategies are covered in the next chapter, which aims to complete the purpose of this section.

Distinguishing the concepts of "action" and "strategy" may help us understand the other side of the game protocol. In brief, action is a basic alternative in the exchange environment, as shown in the game-theoretical structure, which interdependently affects the payoffs of either participant. Strategy is a purposive and outer action, such as promising, threatening, and signing a contract.

The theoretical foundation of this method for the emergence of behaviors mainly rests on the exogenous changes of the preferences of players, which alter the payoff structure. In this domain, a number of authors (e.g., Schelling (1960) with the "commitment mechanism," Lazear (1995) with "culture," Kandel and Lazear (1992) with "feelings" of guilt, and James (2002) with explicit or implicit contracts) have outlined categories of strategies and analyzed how payoff matrixes change according to them. Let us see how a contract promotes trust in barter exchange in order to present the common features of these research works.

Signing an explicit or implicit contract in order to solve the dilemma embedded in exchange is a strategic choice before the transaction. For instance, Chapter 2, section "Trust in current exchange theories" described how an explicit contract facilitates barter exchange. However, here I concentrate on the strategy of using implicit contracts. According to James (2002), "The basic distinction between explicit and implicit contracts is that implicit contracts cannot be enforced by third parties, such as courts" (p. 299). This fact suggests the need for enforcements that come from social sanctions (e.g., exclusion).

The example in Figure 4.2 shows how an implicit contract promotes trust in the one-shot situation of the barter economy. In this case, both players execute a contract, creating a cost c to both, and n (cost of sanctioning) is the effect of both players imposing the social sanction m to collaborate with the defector. However, this changes the payoff environment and endows the solution for exchange in one-shot situations. For example, when value $(a + x - m)$ is equal to zero, and $(a - c)$ is greater than zero, this alters the interactive structure to become a variant of the Stag-Hunt game.

A Stag-Hunt game describes the situation of both hunters being better off through trust (hunting a stag). In a game-theoretical analysis, there are two Nash equilibria, one is a risk-dominant equilibrium (better off but risky) and the other is a payoff-dominant equilibrium (Pareto-inefficient but safe), which

	Trust	Exploitation
Trust	$a - c, a - c$	$-b - c - n, a + x - m$
Exploitation	$a + x - m, -b - c - n$	$0, 0$

Figure 4.2 Barter exchange with an implicit contract ($0 < b \leq a < a + x$, $0 < x, c, n, m$).

results in the question of selecting equilibria. Consider the expectation function to be a solution in this context. It is assumed that the column player with probability $p(0 \leq p \leq 1)$ chooses trust and with $(1 - p)$ selects exploitation. Hence, the payoffs for selecting trust and exploitation for the row player are given by:

$$\pi_{row}^{Trust} = (a-c)p+(-b-c-n)(1-p),$$

$$\pi_{row}^{Exploitation} = (a+x-m)p.$$

When $\pi_{row}^{Trust} > \pi_{row}^{Exploitation} \rightarrow p > (b+c+n)/(b+n+x-m)$, the row player will choose trust. Likewise, the analysis above is similar for the column player.

So far, we have focused on the strategy of signing an explicit contract in one-shot situations, where players can trust one another because of the factors that exogenously change the payoff environment. Although different types of strategies promote trust in one-shot situations, in essence they carry out similar jobs.

In sum, moves and strategies, as two important components of the game protocol, were theoretically introduced in this section to explain why and how trust emerges even if payoff environments are characterized by two-sided variant PD in the barter economy or one-sided variant PD in monetary exchange in one-shot situations. These emphasize the importance of exogenous arrangements on trust in realistic exchange environments. This section thus less explained the nature of the various forms of arrangements rather than extending them. In this sense, it provided the fundamental points for the mechanism design of trust in exchange.

Trust in evolutionary interdependence

Trust can be learned when individuals engage in strategic interactions. For example, it is by seeing other people walk across a rickety bridge that a person trusts that the bridge is safe. Similarly, Peter wants to have dinner out, but he has no idea which restaurant is best. When he walks down the road looking in the windows of restaurants and sees a crowded dining room, he trusts that the restaurant is good and decides to eat there. In both these cases, the significant analytical move is not to estimate what will happen but rather to trust the decisions of others. In some senses, this is not unusual because evidence shows that when people are uncertain about something, they are willing to follow others (Kandori *et al.*, 1993; Weibull, 1998; Nowak *et al.*, 2004; Apesteguia *et al.*, 2007; Fudenberg and Imhof, 2008). This notion provides the foundation to study the emergence of trust in this context, or how imitation promotes trust in a population.

The following section thus serves to enhance theoretical research on imitation by introducing the approach including Moran and pairwise processes. Then, in the section "A model of the emergence of trust in barter exchange," a model is presented that displays the underlying principles for the emergence of trust in this dynamic situation.

Emergence of trust: A model of imitation

The formal concept of imitation from social science is one of the important rules for describing human behaviors. Imitation appears when different types of individuals in interactions cause different payoffs, meaning that anyone might revise his or her strategy according to the person that is performing well. Alternatively, imitation emerges by "learning to do an act from seeing it done" (Thorndike, 1898, p. 50). For example, a baby learns to write by following the ways of his or her parent.

Indeed, imitating trust is not new in economics, but close attention to this concept is rare. One example of imitating trust occurs in friendships. A person's friend often trusts a new friend, which in turn makes it more likely that this person trusts the new friend, too. Similarly, as mentioned earlier, when one notices the emergence of a bank run, such distrust in the bank in question can be imitated. Hence, when people are uncertain about some factor, imitation arises, which activates or inactivates the emergence of trust. This imitation dynamic (see Chapter 3, section "Basic concepts") is expected to facilitate analysis from a theoretical perspective. In this vein, inversely, such thinking is supposed to guide the purpose we chase. Therefore, the study of imitation dynamics allows us to predict the emergence of trust in exchange and provide the sufficient conditions for it.

Theoretical approaches of imitation in the evolutionary domain, such as the pairwise comparison process (Bradley and Terry, 1952), Moran process (Moran, 1962), and Wright–Fisher process (Wright, 1931), originally derived from evolutionary biology by means of EGT. In social science, these methods have been widely applied to explain the emergence of cooperation in the evolutionary domain (e.g., Gintis, 2000; Nowak and Sigmund, 2005). In this part, to extend this approach to studies of trust, I introduce the concepts of the pairwise comparison and Moran processes, which can be applied to the emergence of trust.

Pairwise comparison process

In this process of imitation, two individuals are chosen from the whole population. The first person, A, is dominant and he or she chooses the strategy of the subdominant one (B) with a probability p based on the difference in payoffs, which is given by:

$$p = \frac{1}{1 + e^{-w(\pi_A - \pi_B)}}. \tag{4.1}$$

Hence, the probability p linearly increases with payoff differences, of which parameter w is the intensity of selection, which affects the sensitivity to the payoff comparison. Therefore, when $w \leq 1$, the differences in $\pi_A - \pi_B$ have only a slight effect on the value of p, whereas when $w > 1$, the value of p is largely contingent on them. w can be simply understood as the consideration that the choices of individuals in interactions are not only dependent on a payoff comparison but also rest on other factors such as culture. This helps understand the importance of payoff differences in imitating behaviors; thus, in the ordinary treatment, $w \leq 1$. This equation explains the fact that an individual often imitates other exchange strategies by comparing the payoff difference. For example, one company adopts a strategy that generates great profits, which makes other companies consider imitating. Applied to this research, since the pairwise comparison process conveys a purposive nature of imitation, it aims to explain why people attempt to imitate "trust" in exchange, given that trusting behavior increases payoffs.

Moran process

Several evolutionary studies of the issue of natural selection in different contexts have involved individual and collective interactions, labeled individual and group selection. The applications of natural selection alter considerably, but the Moran process is typically utilized. Its components refer to a selection process where in high probability good behaviors survive over long-run evolutionary processes. This process can be described as follows: in the population, one individual is chosen at random, but proportional to the fitness (i.e., payoffs from interactions) (Traulsen and Hauert, 2009) gives birth to an identical offspring, who then kills the one selected stochastically. This may offer an implication for imitation by imagining that the killed individual shifts to that offspring in the selection process. In this sense, it is similar to the pairwise comparison process through the probabilistic conversion of behaviors in proportion to the payoff differences. Many authors have applied this process to emphasize the fact that behaviors with high payoffs might be copied by others (consider the metaphor of the "invisible hand" in the market). In this specific consideration, the rule from the Moran process – choosing individuals with high payoffs to imitate others – is followed in this study.

Combining the forgoing suggests an imitation dynamic model of trust divided into two processes: choosing individuals with high payoffs to imitate others and carrying out a probabilistic conversion proportional to the payoff differences. One would argue that the consideration of one of these processes is enough; however, the optimization of the method makes a greater relative contribution. Hence, I provide a model to show how trust emerges in the barter economy.

A model of the emergence of trust in barter exchange

The previous section presented an imitation dynamic for the study of the emergence of trust, which is examined in this section. With this consideration, I display a new model and offer sufficient conditions for the dynamic emergence of trust in barter exchange.

As discussed in Chapter 3, I describe the interactive structure of the barter economy below (for details on how to transform a game-theoretical structure into an evolutionary one, see Elsner *et al.*, 2014). Suppose N individuals ($N \geq 2$) are randomly matched in the barter economy, of which i individuals display trusting behavior, labeled the A type, and ($N - i$) individuals follow exploitation, named the B type. This interactive structure suggests that when A encounters types A and B, he or she receives the payoffs a and $-b$, respectively. By contrast, when B encounters types B and A, he or she receives the payoffs 0 and $a + x$, respectively:

$$
\begin{array}{cc}
 & \begin{array}{cc} A & \quad B \end{array} \\
\begin{array}{c} A \\ B \end{array} & \begin{pmatrix} a & -b \\ a+x & 0 \end{pmatrix}
\end{array}
$$

where $0 < a < b < a + x$.

Then, since individuals interact with equal probability, the payoffs for any A and B types from interactions can be determined as follows:

$$
\pi_i^A = \frac{(i-1)a + (N-i)(-b)}{N-1},
$$

$$
\pi_i^B = \frac{i(a+x) + (N-i-1)0}{N-1} = \frac{i(a+x)}{N-1}. \tag{4.2}
$$

Based on the basic setting of the imitation dynamic model, in each time step, choosing an individual M in the population to be the dominant one that imitates others is contingent on the probability proportional to the payoffs. For any A type, this probability can be defined as:

$$\frac{i\pi_i^A}{i\pi_i^A + (N-i)\pi_i^B}. \tag{4.3}$$

For any B type, it is described as:

$$\frac{(N-i)\pi_i^B}{i\pi_i^A + (N-i)\pi_i^B}. \tag{4.4}$$

Second, consider the pairwise comparison process, namely randomly choosing one individual in the population (labeled F) and then for M comparing the payoffs with F, to the extent that M changes his or her type with the following probability:

$$p = \frac{1}{1+e^{-w(\pi_M - \pi_F)}}(w \le 1). \tag{4.5}$$

Hence, in any interaction period, a new A type is transformed from the B types with a transitional probability shown by:

$$I_{i,i+1} = \frac{(N-i)}{\,} \frac{(N-i)\pi_i^B}{i\pi_i^A + (N-i)\pi_i^B} * p_i * \frac{1}{1+e^{-w(\pi_i^B - \pi_i^A)}} \ (p_i = \frac{i}{N}). \tag{4.6}$$

Likewise, A types reduce by a transitional probability of:

$$I_{i,i-1} = \frac{i\pi_i^A}{i\pi_i^A + (N-i)\pi_i^B} * (1-p_i) * \frac{1}{1+e^{-w(\pi_i^A - \pi_i^B)}}. \tag{4.7}$$

Thus, when

$$\frac{I_{i,i+1}}{I_{i,i-1}} > 1, \tag{4.8}$$

imitation will support the emergence of A types (i.e., the emergence of trust). By substituting equations (4.6) and (4.7) into (4.8), this can be rewritten as:

$$\frac{(N-i)\pi_i^B}{i\pi_i^A} * \frac{i}{N-i} * \frac{\dfrac{1}{1+e^{-w(\pi_i^B - \pi_i^A)}}}{\dfrac{1}{1+e^{-w(\pi_i^A - \pi_i^B)}}} > 1$$

$$\frac{\pi_i^B}{\pi_i^A} * \frac{\dfrac{1}{1+e^{-w(\pi_i^B - \pi_i^A)}}}{\dfrac{1}{1+e^{-w(\pi_i^A - \pi_i^B)}}} > 1. \tag{4.9}$$

For $0 < w \leq 1$, $\dfrac{1}{1 + e^{\mp w(\pi_i^A - \pi_i^B)}} \cong [\dfrac{1}{2} \pm \dfrac{w}{4}(\pi_i^A - \pi_i^B)]$ (Traulsen *et al.*, 2007).

Thus, equation (4.9) can be described as follows:

$$\pi_i^B [\dfrac{1}{2} - \dfrac{w}{4}(\pi_i^A - \pi_i^B)] > \pi_i^A [\dfrac{1}{2} + \dfrac{w}{4}(\pi_i^A - \pi_i^B)]$$

$$(\pi_i^B - \pi_i^A) [\dfrac{1}{2} + \dfrac{w}{4}(\pi_i^B + \pi_i^A)] > 0. \tag{4.10}$$

Finally, substituting equation (4.2) into (4.10) shows that the first part $(\pi_i^B - \pi_i^A)$ is above zero, meaning that it can be neglected. Thus, the final outcome can be written as follows:

$$(2 - 2bw)N + (2a + x + b)i - 2aw - 2 > 0. \tag{4.11}$$

So far, we have assessed the possible emergence of trust in the context of imitation dynamics, where the conditions are given. In other words, when $(2 - 2bw)N + (2a + x + b)i - 2aw - 2 > 0$, the market supports the emergence of trust in barter exchange through imitation. For monetary and Internet exchanges, trust in imitation dynamics is not given. This may be a research direction for future studies. However, the present study aims to illustrate a theoretical method that considers the imitation process on the emergence of trust in exchange systems. In this sense, it extends the findings of previous studies of exchange and trust.

Of course, more complicated cases exist in which to consider imitation dynamics. For example, when discussing immigration, the next generation of the population may have a different composition, implying that the imitation dynamics of trust are additionally complicated. Indeed, although exchange is considered to be stable and smooth in the cases examined herein, any turbulence can be treated as noise, which is explored in Chapter 6.

Summary

This chapter explained how trust emerges in behavioral and evolutionary interdependences in the system of trust. In behavioral interdependence, trust in interactions is composed of expectation, reason, and calculation according to the findings of previous studies and prior models of the emergence of trust. From an exogenous perspective, the section "Emergence of trust: Exogenous arrangements" showed how exogenous arrangements (e.g., game protocols) trigger the emergence of trust, which then serves as a foundation for future mechanism design. In evolutionary interdependence, the function of imitation was emphasized and a model of the emergence of trust in barter exchange was presented. This model painted a picture that people that imitate perform best, thereby promoting the emergence of trust under certain conditions.

References

Apesteguia, J., Huck, S. and Oechssler, J. 2007. Imitation: Theory and Experimental Evidence. *Journal of Economic Theory*, 136(1), 217–235.

Axelrod, R. 1984. *The Evolution of Cooperation*. New York, NY: Basic Books.

Bigley, G.A., Pearce, J.L. 1998. Straining for Shared Meaning in Organization Science: Problems of Trust and Distrust. *Academy of Management Review*, 23(3), 405–421.

Binmore, K. 1993. Bargaining and Morality. In: Gauthier, D., Sugden, R. (Eds), *Rationality, Justice and the Social Contract: Themes from "Morals by Agreement"*. New York, NY: Harvester Wheatsheaf, 131–156.

Bradley, R.A., Terry, M.E. 1952. Rank Analysis of Incomplete Block Designs, I: The Method of Paired Comparisons. *Biometrika*, 39, 324–345.

Bruni, L., Sugden, R. 2000. Moral Canals: Trust and Social Capital in the Work of Humer, Smith and Genovesi. *Economics and Philosophy*, 16(1), 21–45.

Coleman, J.S. 1990. *Foundations of Social Theory*. Cambridge, MA: Harvard University Press.

Deutsch, M. 1960. Trust, Trustworthiness, and F-scale. *Journal of Abnormal and Social Psychology*, 61, 138–140.

Elsner, W., Heinrich, T., Schwardt, H. 2014. *An Introduction to the Microeconomics of Complexity*. San Diego, CA: Elsevier Inc.

Elsner, W., Schwardt, H. 2014. Trust and Arena Size: Expectations, Institutions, and General Trust, and Critical Population and Group Sizes. *Journal of Institutional Economics*, 10(1), 107–134.

Fudenberg, D., Imhof, L.A. 2008. Monotone Imitation Dynamics in Large Populations. *Journal of Economic Theory*, 140, 229–245.

Gambetta, D. 1988. Can We Trust in Trust? In: Gambetta, D. (Ed.), *Trust: Making and Breaking Cooperative Relations*. New York, NY: University of Oxford, 213–237.

Gauthier, D. 1986. *Morals by Agreement*. Oxford: Oxford University Press.

Gintis, H. 2000. *Game Theory Evolving*. Princeton, NJ: Princeton University Press.

Granovetter, M.S. 1985. Economic Action and Social Structure: The Problem of Embeddedness. *American Journal of Sociology*, 91, 481–510.

Greif, A. 1989. Reputation and Coalitions in Medieval Trade: Evidence on the Maghribi Traders. *Journal of Economic History*, 49(4), 857–991.

Hardin, R. 2006. *Trust: Key Concepts*. Cambridge, UK: Polity Press.

Hirshleifer, J. 1999. There are Many Evolutionary Pathways to Cooperation. *Journal of Bioecoomics*, 1(1), 73–93.

Hollis, M. 1998. *Trust Within Reason*. Cambridge, UK: Cambridge University Press.

Hume, D. 1740. *A Treatise of Human Nature*. Oxford: Oxford University Press.

James, H.S. Jr 2002. The Trust Paradox: A Survey of Economic Inquiries into the Nature of Trust and Trustworthiness. *Journal of Economic Behavior & Organization*, 47(3), 291–307.

Kandel, E., Lazear, E.P. 1992. Peer Pressure and Partnerships. *Journal of Political Economy*, 100(4), 801–817.

Kandori, M., Mailath, G.J., Rob, M.R. 1993. Learning, Mutation, and Long Run Equilibria in Games. *Econometrica*, 61, 29–56.

Lazear, E.P. 1995. Corporate Culture and the Diffusion of Values. In: Horst, S. (Ed.), *Trends in Business Organization: Do Participation and Cooperation Increase Competitiveness?* Tuebingen: JCB Mohr.

Macaulay, S. 1963. Non-Contractual Relations in Business: A Preliminary Study. *American Sociological Review*, 28(1), 55–67.

Möllering, G. 2006. *Trust: Reason, Routine, Reflexivity*. Oxford: Elsevier.

Moran, P.A.P. 1962. *The Statistical Processes of Evolutionary Theory*. Oxford: Clarendon Press.

Nowak, M., Sigmund, K. 2005. Evolution of Indirect Reciprocity. *Nature*, 437, 1291–1298.

Nowak, M.A., Sasaki, A., Taylor, C., Fudenberg, D. 2004. Emergence of Cooperation and Evolutionary Stability in Finite Populations. *Nature*, 428, 646–650.

Putnam, R. 1993. *Making Democracy Work*. Princeton, NJ: Princeton University Press.

Schelling, T.C. 1960. *The Strategy of Conflict*. New York, NY: Oxford University Press.

Smith, A. 1776. *An Inquiry into the Nature and Causes of the Wealth of Nations*. Oxford: Oxford University Press.

Thorndike, E.L. 1898. *Animal Intelligence: An Experimental Study of the Associative Processes in Animals* (Psychological Review, Monograph Supplements, No. 8). New York, NY: Macmillan.

Traulsen, A., Pacheco, J.M., Nowak, M.A. 2007. Pairwise Comparison and Selection Temperature in Evolutionary Game Dynamics. *Journal of Theoretical Biology*, 246, 522–529.

Weibull, J.W. 1998. *What Have We Learned from Evolutionary Game Theory So Far?* Research Institute of Industrial Economics. Working Papers 487, Research Institute of Industrial Economics. Available at: http://ideas.repec.org/p/hhs/iuiwop/0487.html.

Wright, S. 1931. Evolution in Mendelian Populations. *Genetics*, 16, 97–159.

5 Evolution and the stability of trust

Before exploring the evolution and stability of trust within micro-to-macro and macro-to-micro transitions in the system of trust, it is helpful to illustrate a trend based on data taken from the *World Values Survey* (available at: http://www.worldvaluessurvey.org/wvs.jsp). Figure 5.1 shows that the level of trust (*general trust*) in Germany and Britain strongly fluctuated from 1980 to 1999, suggesting that while trust declines in the long run, it is stable in the short term.

Under such a circumstance, we may question the principle behind the evolution and stability of trust, namely how trust evolves in interactive

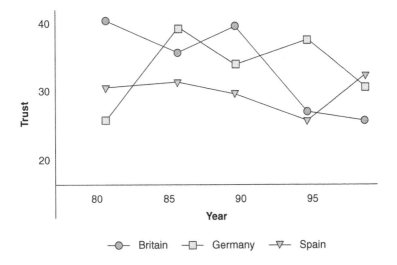

Figure 5.1 Levels of general trust changing over time.

Source: World Values Survey (http://www.worldvaluessurvey.org/wvs.jsp).

interactions and where it is stable. If, in light of the theory displayed, the emergence of interactive structures provided by exchange systems influences changes in trust, the essence of trust phenomena is likely to be revealed by demonstrating the dynamic way in which trust is placed in interactive structures (i.e., the co-evolving theory of exchange systems and trust). Hence, this chapter examines these factors in the framework mentioned in Chapter 1 by performing the evolutionary approach, showing its dynamic features and drawing conclusions on the impact of exchange systems on trust when interactive structures are distinct.

The section "The phenomena of the co-evolution of trust and exchange systems: Trust in barter and monetary economies," based on historical evidence, examines the phenomena of the evolution of trust in an interactive context (i.e., at a country level). It demonstrates that barter exchange decreases trust, while monetary exchange makes trust fluctuate over time. With this recognition, the following section "Micro-to-macro transition of trust in exchange systems: Trust in different interactive structures and populations" models the evolutionary process of trust in barter, monetary, and Internet exchanges by using the evolutionary approach, which focuses on the emergence of interactive structures and applies replicator dynamics to illustrate the dynamic feature of the micro-to-macro transition of trust. To investigate the stability of these processes, stability analysis is provided in the section "Stability of trust."

The phenomena of the co-evolution of trust and exchange systems: Trust in barter and monetary economies

In Chapter 2, it was argued that the evolution of exchange systems may bring together distinctive interactive trust phenomena as well as real phenomena that are never referenced. This section thus provides historical evidence that explains this point and presents relevant models.

Breakdown of trust in bartering: Evidence from barter economies, 1991–1999

Since the early 1990s, some of the countries of the former Soviet Union (e.g., Russia and Ukraine) have experienced a quick transition from central regulation to a deregulated capitalist economy. These transition economies have been examined in mainstream economic studies to understand the impact of central planning and market economies on growth. However, while transition economies are generally considered to be moving from a planned to a market economy, they are rarely recognized as shifting from a process of bartering to one of monetary exchange. According to the *World Business Environment Survey*, 20 transition economies are characterized by the development of bartering, with bartering in Russia accounting for 60 percent of GDP in 1998 (European Bank for Reconstruction and Development, 1999). Large barter economies typically have a lower level of trust, as reflected in the data from the *World Values Survey* (about general trust) presented in Figure 5.2. Intuitively, this finding signifies that when bartering is prevalent, trust erodes over time.

Bartering creates a trust problem because it is difficult to measure the quality of commodities owing to asymmetric information, which encourages opportunistic behavior. Chapter 2 stated that bartering under such circumstances leads to an interactive structure characterized by double defection in which the agents involved in exchange are prone to cheating, rather than trusting, which serves as a disincentive to trust building. With regard to this point, at an aggregated level, it is inferred that the macro status of the system is enveloped in an atmosphere of distrust.

Russia rapidly developed its barter trade after the collapse of the former Soviet Union. Between 1990 and 2000, the country's "goods for goods"

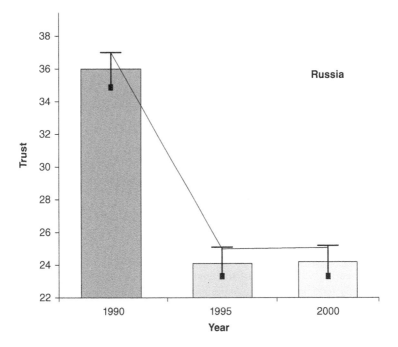

Figure 5.2 General trust in Russia.

Source: World Value Survey (http://www.worldvaluessurvey.org/wvs.jsp).

exchange model gradually replaced the "money for goods" model and all Russian transactions began to be organized through bartering, causing the breakdown of trust (Johnson *et al.*, 1997).

Figure 5.2 shows that the level of trust declined from 37 percent of general trust in 1990 to 24 percent in 1995 before stabilizing between 1995 and 2000. This lower level of trust in Russia co-evolved with the development of bartering in Russia from 1991 to 2000. Russia is not a special case, however, and other transition countries (e.g., Slovenia, Moldova, Croatia, Slovakia, and Ukraine) show a similar low average level of trust compared with developed monetary economies (see Figure 5.3). In a broader sense, the barter economy thus creates a decline of trust.

The impact of bartering on trust can also be seen by the positive relationship between barter share and trust. Barter share is a basic indicator of the relative contribution of bartering to GDP in a country, allowing us to compare the proportions of non-monetary and monetary economies in one country over time. The World Bank surveyed the barter shares in 20 transition economies in 1999, most of which are presented in Table 5.1 (note: countries lacking

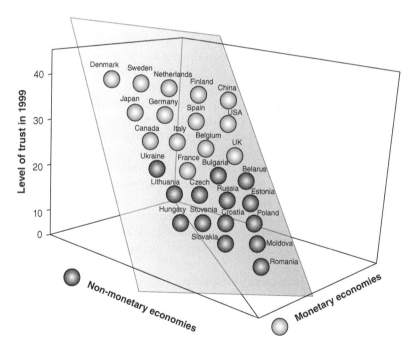

Figure 5.3 Trust in non-monetary and monetary economies (1999).

Source: General Trust in World Values Survey (http://www.worldvaluessurvey.org/wvs.jsp); World Business Environment Survey, World Bank-EBRD (1999).

Table 5.1 Barter shares and generalized trust in different countries in 1999

Countries	Barter share in 1999 (%)	Generalized trust in 1999 (%)
Belarus	4.2	26.8
Bulgaria	4.0	26.8
Croatia	32.8	20.5
Czech Republic	3.3	24.6
Estonia	4.1	23.5
Hungary	0.8	22.4
Lithuania	2.8	25.9
Moldova	26.3	14.6
Poland	4.7	18.4
Romania	7.3	10.1
Russia	24.1	24.0
Slovakia	19.2	15.9
Slovenia	16.3	21.7
Ukraine	24.0	27.8

Source: World Business Environment Survey, World Bank-EBRD (1999); World Values Survey (http://www.worldvaluessurvey.org/wvs.jsp).

data about general trust are not presented in the table). The change in barter shares is presumed to co-evolve with trust, which implies an orientation for future studies provided more data are made available.

Figure 5.4 shows that barter share influences levels of trust across countries, which suggests that barter exchange does not support trust. The figure demonstrates that in 1999 barter shares had a linearly negative correlation with trust; in other words, as barter shares increase, indicating that more people engage in bartering, trust decreases. It should however be noted that this evidence is too weak to support the argument because of data limitations. Nevertheless, over time, history reopens a window for us to test this issue. In any case, it is clear that bartering decreases trust in largely interactive processes, especially when institutions are unstable. In sum, the interdependent structure of bartering does not support trust.

Trust phenomena in monetary economies

Monetary systems concern how people use money for exchange and how the two roles of buyers and sellers interact. While in a barter economy, it is difficult to meet "occasionally double wants," in monetary exchange no such problem exists. Numerous empirical and theoretical studies have been related to topics such as inflation rates, transaction costs, and prices. These concerns often, however, tend to make us ignore the basic problem of trust in exchange.

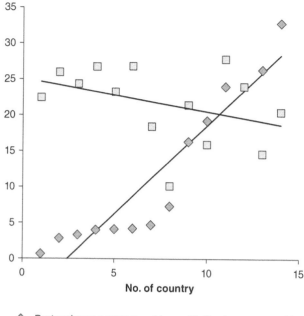

◇ Barter shares across countries   ☐ Trust across countries

Figure 5.4 Barter share and trust across countries in 1999.

The monetary system affects trust in a society. Simmel (1990) presented a special account of exchange as a direct bond of individuals in which trust is embedded in the medium of exchange (i.e., money). The implication of this account is that societal cohesiveness is contingent on the achievement of monetary exchange. However, this process of trust is affected by inflation, which devalues money, diminishes trust, and makes members of society rush to purchase. The best-known argument here was by Smith (1776), who believed that the emergence of monetary exchange improves efficiency but enhances self-interest and greed, leading to a problem of trust. Similarly, Skaggs (1998) argued that money's emergence leads to a series of credits either between or among individuals or organizations: "Individuals possessing financial wealth were willing to entrust their money to those in need of liquid funds in exchange for promises to repay the loan principal plus interest in the future" (p. 453). This results in networks of debt across the system and supports trust in society.

Hence, the emergence of monetary exchange, albeit as a medium to help overcome the problem of "occasional double wants" and difficulty

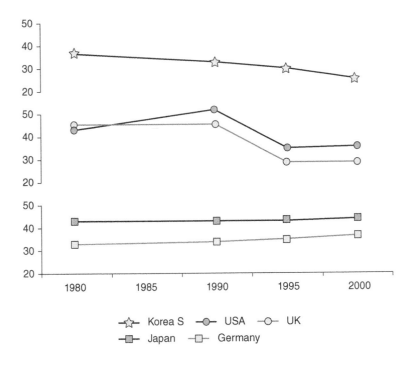

Figure 5.5 Varieties of changes in trust in monetary economies.
Source: World Values Survey (http://www.worldvaluessurvey.org/wvs.jsp).

in evaluating the actual values of goods in bartering, results in a one-sided variant PD game (see Chapter 2, section "Trust in the evolution of exchange systems: Interdependence structures and populations in the system of trust"). Although governing one-sided defection is less sophisticated compared with the two-sided one, even nowadays, it is almost unavoidable in monetary exchange. Consumers are often worried about being cheated after paying for goods, as assessing actual quality and value is difficult. Moreover, sellers may include fake ingredients in commodities in order to maximize profits (e.g., poisoned eggs) and design unreasonable contracts that aim to exploit (e.g., handy contracts), which deteriorate trust. Thus, consumers are likely to be careful, especially when dealing with strangers. In this vein, trust is affected by the emergence of interactive structures perceived as a one-sided variant PD game.

In sum, barter exchange does not support trust because of the structure of two-sided variant PD games, which results in the breakdown of trust, whereas in the monetary system, one-sided variant PD games produce different pictures of trust in a largely interactive context (see Figure 5.5). What is remarkable in Figure 5.5 is that the change in trust over time characterized by a variety of monetary economies is clear: the USA and UK are represented by an arched shape, Japan and Germany have a gradually increasing one, and South Korea has a gradually decreasing shape. These trends imply that noise (e.g., institutions) in monetary systems affects the evolution of trust more than in barter systems because of the presence of interdependent structures. In other words, the evolution of trust changes with noise over time to a relatively easy degree because of the existence of one-sided PD structures. Moreover, these theoretical outcomes help us realize that the explanation of the change in trust at the country level may have a new argument based on an interactive perspective, rather than just reflected by GDP (e.g., Knack and Philip, 1997) from an empirical perspective.

Micro-to-macro transition of trust in exchange systems: Trust in different interactive structures and populations

Trust is a system of micro-level individual behaviors in an interactive structure interdependent of the macro-level state (Coleman, 1990). This simple summary from Coleman highlights two important points. First, the state of trust in a society is an aggregated outcome of all micro-level individual behaviors. Second, the interactive structure is crucial to how individuals act trustworthily in the process.

Exchange systems provide distinct interactive structures and populations for the *system of trust* when micro-level behaviors match the micro-to-macro transition process (see Chapter 2, section "Trust in the evolution of exchange systems: Interdependence structures and populations in the system of trust"). For example, in barter exchange, there exists a symmetric structure (i.e., two-sided variant PD across homogeneous matches), in monetary exchange, there exists an asymmetric structure (i.e., one-sided variant PD across heterogeneous matches), and in Internet exchange, there exists an asymmetric structure with enforcement across heterogeneous matches. Thus, two logical questions arise: how does trust evolve in a specific "matching structure and population" and what is the approach in these explorations?

Chapter 3 described how purposive behaviors by agents evolve in an interactive process from a micro-level structure to the macro state of a system: EGT. This notion has long been popular in evolutionary studies (e.g., Young, 1998; Weibull, 1998; Santos *et al.*, 2006). In this section, one of the basic but most important evolutionary dynamics in this approach, namely replicator dynamics, is used to show the evolution of trust in exchange systems provided the population is infinite and well-mixed in the interactive process (see section "The phenomena of the co-evolution of trust and exchange systems: Trust in barter and monetary economies" above).

In a general setting, the principles for analyzing these behaviors in an interactive structure through replicator equations are required to identify whether the structure is asymmetric or symmetric (Cressman, 1992). Although this point has already been explained in Chapter 2, section "Systems of trust: Elements, interdependences, and micro-to-macro/macro-to-micro transitions", I repeat it here to help clarify their differences and provide a foundation for building the model. For simplicity, to understand the differences between symmetric and asymmetric structures based on EGT, Maynard Smith (1974) used the metaphor of "symmetry evolution" in the animal world, meaning that two individuals that display the same behaviors in a single animal species conflict. This notion can be understood by the examples of lions conflicting to obtain food and male chimpanzees battling to breed. Naturally, by contrast, in most cases the structure has two (asymmetric) roles such as male–female, worker–queen, and parent–offspring (Gaunersdorfer *et al.*, 1991). Based on this analysis, the main mode of identification is simply how many roles exist when they match.

Based on the foregoing, the evolution of trust in the barter economy is symmetric in a homogeneous population (see Figure 5.6). Specifically, an emergent structure in the barter economy is a two-sided variant PD game in which both sides have the same strategies (either trust or defection) and one role is involved. When bartering, two pairwise partners are both buyers and sellers simultaneously, selling commodities and obtaining goods. Moreover, the quality and actual value of these goods are perceived subjectively, which could benefit opportunists in the exchange process. Hence, the presence of

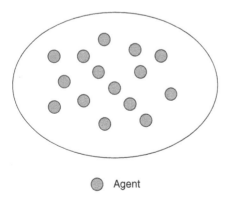

⬤ Agent

Figure 5.6 A homogeneous population in the symmetric evolution of trust (the system of trust in barter exchange).

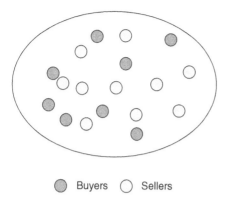

Buyers ○ Sellers

Figure 5.7 Two groups in heterogeneous populations involving the asymmetric evolution of trust (the system of trust in monetary exchange).

this "invisible hand" in barter exchange, where defection is preferable as long as uncertainties exist, diminishes trust. To confirm this expectation, I express this idea through replicator dynamics in this section.

Compared with barter exchange, the evolution of trust embedded in monetary exchange is asymmetric in a heterogeneous population. Here, the emergent structure is asymmetric in which one individual involved in interactions is the buyer and the other is the seller. This phenomenon reflects the influence of the intervention of money in the exchange process, which makes some individuals independent of the population (i.e., some engage in selling and others in buying). A heterogeneous population in this exchange is presented in Figure 5.7.

As defined in Chapter 2, buyers enjoy better quality and an accurate quantity of goods, and thus they decide whom to trust in exchange, whereas sellers pursue self-interests. The evolution of trust thus is to some degree contingent on this asymmetric context within these two groups.

A similar analysis is suitable for the evolution of trust in Internet exchange, which is an asymmetric evolution in heterogeneous populations, but with "enforcements" from the platform on which exchange is directly based (see Figure 5.8). According to Figure 5.8, if sellers choose to exploit the trust of the trusting, the underlying punishment will be raised from these platforms. For example, defectors may face a downgraded credit rating or exclusion from the trading platforms. In this view, when these enforcements run into the emergent structure of Internet exchange, the incentive structure changes and this influences the evolution of trust.

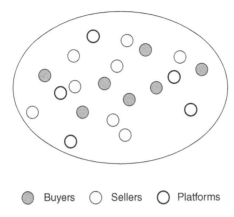

Buyers ⬤   Sellers ◯   Platforms ◯

Figure 5.8 Two groups involved in the asymmetric evolution with enforcements (the system of trust in Internet exchange).

From an evolutionary perspective, "emergent matching structures and populations" are supposed to affect the evolution of trust in interactions. Considering the above characteristics, replicator dynamic models can be built to describe the micro-to-macro transition of trust in these emergent structures and populations.

Replicator dynamics of trust in a homogeneous population: Barter exchange

The interactive structures in barter, monetary, and Internet exchanges were shown in Chapter 2, section "Trust in the evolution of exchange systems: Interdependence structures and populations in the system of trust." In this subsection, these are linked to replicator dynamic models to display the evolution of trust over time when emergent structures are considered. Let us first model the evolution of trust in barter exchange (Figure 2.7). According to the definition of the barter economy and previous analysis, in a large homogeneous population with symmetric interactions, suppose m individuals playing a trust strategy and $(1 - m)$ ones following an exploitation strategy engage in barter exchange. As the evolutionary model in Chapter 3, section "Evolutionary modeling" illustrated, the expected payoffs of individual i under trust and exploit strategies are given by:

$$\pi_i^{Trust} = ma + (-b)(1 - m) = ma - b + bm, \tag{5.1}$$

$$\pi_i^{Exploit} = (a + x)m + 0(1 - m) = am + xm. \tag{5.2}$$

Then, the average expected payoff of the collective is:

$$\pi^{Average} = (ma - b + bm)m + (am + xm)(1 - m)$$
$$= (a + x - b)m + (b - x)m^2. \tag{5.3}$$

Hence, combining equations (5.1) and (5.2) leads to:

$$\dot{m} = \pi_i^{Trust} - \pi^{average}$$

$$\rightarrow \dot{m} = m(1 - m)[(b - x)m - b]. \tag{5.4}$$

By simulating equation (5.4), the evolution of trust over time is shown in Figure 5.9. This figure illustrates two points. First, the relationship between barter exchange and the evolution of trust shows that individuals in barter exchange reduce their use of a trust strategy over time (based on the simulations, this reduction occurs regardless of the initial conditions). Second, the outcome meets our theoretical expectation: barter exchange strongly leads

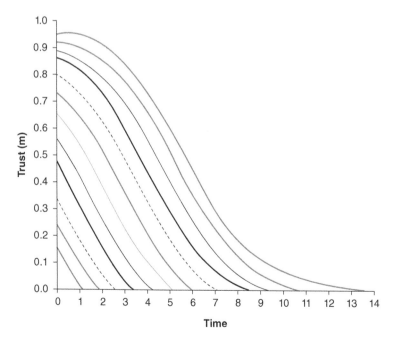

Figure 5.9 Dynamic processes of the evolution of trust in barter exchange. Initial conditions: $a = 2$, $b = 0$, $x = 1$. (Different starting values for m).

to the breakdown of trust. This helps explain why transition countries present lower levels of trust as their barter economies have developed over time. Therefore, our theoretical conclusion in this part is that barter exchange does not support trust: even though most people trust each other in bartering at the beginning, trust decreases gradually over time.

Replicator dynamics of trust in a heterogeneous population: Monetary exchange

Figure 5.7 shows that two randomly matched groups exist in monetary exchange in a heterogeneous population. At the beginning, one group includes buyers n that follow a trust strategy and $(1 - n)$ that adopt a distrust strategy, while the other incorporates sellers l pursuing honor and $(1 - l)$ pursuing exploit. The interactive structure is the same as that in Figure 2.9. Thus, the expected payoffs of buyer i following the trust and distrust strategies are given by:

$$\pi_i^{Trust} = al - b(1-l) = (a+b)l - b, \tag{5.5}$$

$$\pi_i^{Distrust} = 0. \tag{5.6}$$

It follows that the average expected payoff of the group of buyers is:

$$\pi_{group}^{buyer} = n\pi_i^{Trust} + (1-n)\pi_i^{Distrust} = (a+b)nl - bn. \tag{5.7}$$

Therefore, the replicator dynamic equation of the trusting buyers group is:

$$\dot{n} = (\pi_i^{Trust} - \pi_{group}^{buyer}) = n(1-n)[(a+b)l - b]. \tag{5.8}$$

Similarly, the replicator dynamic equation of the honor strategy in the seller group is:

$$\dot{i} = l(1-l)[(f - x)n - f]. \tag{5.9}$$

As before, by simulating equations (5.8) and (5.9), the replicator dynamics of trust and honor are demonstrated in Figure 5.10.

We can understand the characteristics of the evolution of trust in monetary exchange over time (i.e., the micro-to-macro transition of trust in a system of trust) by simulating equations (5.8) and (5.9) and thereby contrasting them with those in barter exchange. The evolution of trust in the monetary system is dependent on the number of sellers that apply an honor strategy. When the number of such sellers is higher than those that adopt a trust strategy in

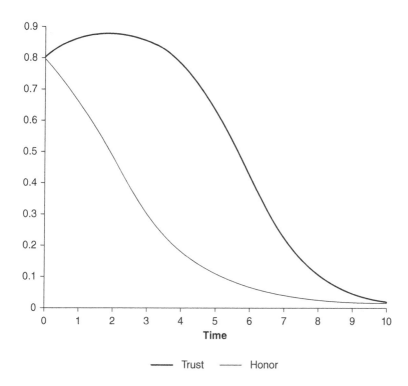

Figure 5.10 Dynamic processes of the evolution of trust and honor in the monetary system. Initial condition $n = 0.8$ and $l = 0.8$, and $a = 1$, $b = 1$, $x = 0.8$, $f = 0.3$.

the buyer group at the beginning of evolution, the shape of the evolution of trust becomes arched over time. That is, it increases first and then declines (see Figure 5.10). This difference is lower than the number of trusting buyers, whose shape is a slope decreasing over time (as in the barter economy). These outcomes partly explain the trust phenomena in monetary economies (see section "Trust phenomena in monetary economies"), namely that various changes in trust exist in monetary exchange because a monetary system can support the evolution of trust in certain periods and under certain conditions.

Replicator dynamics of trust in a heterogeneous population with enforcements: Internet exchange

Similar to monetary exchange, in Internet exchange, it is assumed that two groups exist in an asymmetric interaction. The first group, buyers, includes

g players who adopt a trust strategy and $(1 - g)$ players who pursue a distrust strategy. The other group, sellers, contains k players that follow an honor strategy, and $(1 - k)$ that choose to exploit. The incentive structure is based on that in Figure 2.11. Hence, the expected payoffs of player i following the trust and distrust strategies are indicated by:

$$\pi_i^{Trust} = ak - b(1-k) = (a+b)k - b, \tag{5.10}$$

$$\pi_i^{Distrust} = 0. \tag{5.11}$$

It follows that the expected payoff of the group of buyers is:

$$\pi_{group}^{buyer} = g\pi_i^{Trust} + (1-g)\pi_i^{Distrust} = (a+b)kg - bg. \tag{5.12}$$

Thus, the replicator equation of trust in the group of buyers is:

$$\dot{g} = g(\pi_i^{Trust} - \pi_{group}^{buyer}) = g(1-g)[(a+b)k - b]. \tag{5.13}$$

Similarly, the replicator equation of honor in the seller group is:

$$\dot{k} = k(1-k)[(m+f-x)g - f]. \tag{5.14}$$

Before simulating equations (5.13) and (5.14), the effect of m in the inter-active structure is taken into account, as the incentive structure is likely to alter because of the change in m. When $m < x$ (see Figure 2.10), Internet exchange presents a structure in which a single defection by the seller takes advantage of choosing honor in the interaction, indicating that the results of this simulation of the evolution of trust are identical to those in monetary exchange. When $m > x$, buyers are uncertain about the choices of sellers and vice versa (for more details about such a mixed strategy, see Schelling, 1960). Here, setting $m > x$ for the simulation of the equations is considered. The results below suggest that the evolution of trust in Internet exchange has two main outcomes depending on the different values of g, k, a, b, m, f, and x, namely surviving or extinguishing, even though the shape of the evolution of trust over time differs.

Figure 5.11 demonstrates that the evolution of trust in Internet exchange can produce either negative or positive consequences because of the combination of parameters (e.g., k, g, m, x, and f). The concrete relationships among them are shown in section "Stability of trust" below. This finding indicates that trust can succeed in the long run in some cases, suggesting Internet exchange endogenously underpins trust when the conditions of a certain combination of parameters are met.

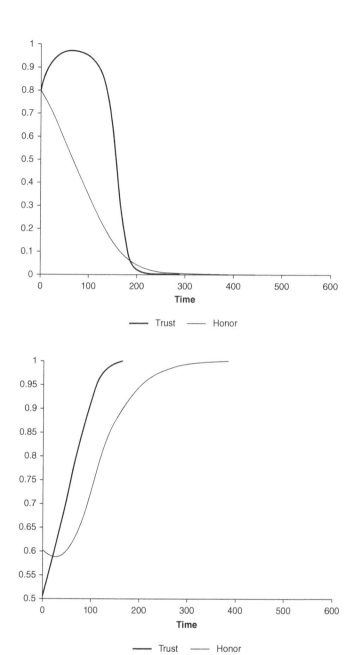

Figure 5.11 Dynamic processes of the evolution of trust in the Internet system. (a) Initial conditions $k = 0.8$ and $g = 0.8$, and $a = 1, b = 1, m = 0.9, x = 0.8, f = 0.1$. (b) Initial conditions $k = 0.6$ and $g = 0.5$, and $a = 1, b = 1, m = 0.9, x = 0.8, f = 0.4$. (c) Initial conditions $k = 0.6$ and $g = 0.4$, and $a = 1, b = 1, m = 0.9, x = 0.8, f = 0.4$. (d) Initial conditions $k = 0.6$ and $g = 0.3$, and $a = 1, b = 1, m = 0.9, x = 0.8, f = 0.4$.

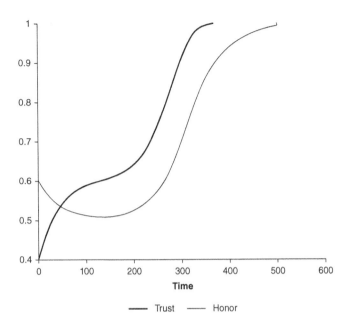

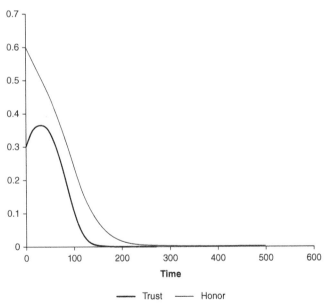

Figure 5.11 (continued)

Stability of trust

Trust is commonly believed to be a fragile thing in transactions, according to Dasgupta (2000), among other scholars. Given the existence of bank runs, panic buying, and so forth, trust is seemingly more collectively unstable. Yet, such negative comments about the stability of trust overlook the fact that it tends to survive in a system that comprises individuals who possess distinct incentives and thus display various behaviors.

Recall that in the analysis of the micro-to-macro transition of trust in a system of trust, various trajectories appear because of the interactive structures in exchange systems (e.g., barter and monetary exchanges). Metaphorically, this is like a ball rolling down different slopes, but the places where it stops in the short- and long-term are not yet known.

Bendor and Swistak (1997) also used the metaphor of ball and slopes to reconsider the standpoint that trust is fragile and collectively unstable in nature. It is easy to understand that exchange systems cause this fragility intrinsically. Imagine that exchange systems are viewed as different slopes and the ball is seen as trust. It is taken for granted that different slopes are likely to provide distinct places for the ball to stop. Those stable stopping points reflect the ability to resist turbulence, both internal and external, indicating the stability of a system.

Figure 5.12 illustrates three examples of these stable stopping points on different slopes. When the ball rests at the first stable point, it has weak stability: although slight turbulence pushes it up because of the original state, the ball is unstable as small disturbances act on it to break it away from that point. When the ball rests at the second stable point, a slight disturbance cannot shift it from there, implying strong stability. Finally, when the ball rests at the third stable point, a slight force will push it down (instability). Intuitively, whether trust is stable is contingent on the points given by systems. Logically, therefore, these descriptions offer enough space to examine how exchange systems exogenously affect the stability of trust, rather than considering trust to be endogenously unstable.

Figure 5.12 highlights an important gap in the body of knowledge on the stability of trust. Thus far, no framework has explained how trust is stable against the inevitable disturbances subjected to exchange systems. This section focuses on bridging this gap through the application of stability analysis under the evolutionary approach.

Considering the above, this subsection is organized as follows. The first section considers ESS to be a cutoff point by examining how exchange systems affect the stability of trust in a static prediction. The next section "The stability analysis of trust in exchange systems: A dynamic prediction" elaborates on the concept of the steady state by using replicator dynamics to describe the stability of trust in a dynamic prediction. Finally, I summarize

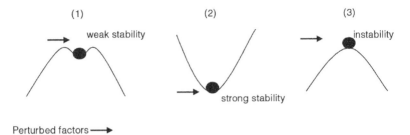

Figure 5.12 Systems and stability points.

the main points in this section and offer suggestions for future studies of the stability of trust.

The stability analysis of trust in exchange systems: A static prediction

ESS

ESS, as a key concept in EGT, was first introduced by Maynard Smith and Price (1973) to analyze population dynamics in symmetric games. Later, Selten (1980) used ESS in asymmetric games as a robust means to reflect the ability of a strategy against a small proportion of invaders in a large population. A strategy is said to be evolutionarily stable if a positive invasion barrier exists that makes it obtain a higher payoff than that of the invasion strategy, when the share of invaders is lower than this barrier (Weibull, 1995).

One straightforward interpretation of ESS is as follows. In a large population, invaders that are displaying distinct types of behaviors join the population. If all the original individuals can obtain a higher payoff than that of invaders under an invasion barrier (a proportion of the population), they rationally play the original strategy rather than selecting the strategy of the invaders (i.e., they are stable).

Invasion barriers under the concept of stability are similar to the metaphor in Figure 5.12: the shapes of the slopes in systems resist turbulence. The scale of an invasion barrier thus helps define the robustness of stability (i.e., weak, strong, instability) and shows how exchange systems affect the stability of trust in different ways. Let us now define these concepts and further analyze the stability of trust in exchange systems.

ESSs in the barter economy: A symmetric interactive structure

Assume that in a large population, ε frequencies of mutant strategy $y \in \Delta$ and $(1 - \varepsilon)$ of individuals that follow strategy $x \in \Delta$ exist. Then, the composition of the population is g = ∈y+ (1 − ∈)x, ∈ ∈(0, 1). In each time step, individuals play a two-person symmetric game when they randomly meet. $E(x, g)$ and $E(y, g)$ are the respective functions of the actual payoffs of an individual who undertakes strategies x and y when he or she encounters g. The formal concept of the stability of a strategy is thus defined as follows:

Definition 5.1 (Weibull, 1995, p. 36, also see section "Basic concepts"). *$x \in \Delta$ is an ESS if for every strategy $y \neq x$ there exists some $\bar{\in}_y \in (0,1)$ such that inequality 5.15 holds for all $\in \in (0, \bar{\in}_y)$,*

$$E[x, \varepsilon y + (1 - \varepsilon)x] > E[y, \varepsilon y + (1 - \varepsilon)x]. \tag{5.15}$$

Let $\lim_{\bar{\in}_y \to 1} \in$ denote the maximum value of $\in$ when $\bar{\in}_y$ approaches one. This means that in a large population of n individuals, the value of $\in$ is equal to $(n-1)/n$ at the maximum (if two strategies exist). Instead, $\lim_{\varepsilon \to 0} \in$ signifies the minimum value of $\in$ when $\bar{\in}_y$ approaches zero, which suggests that $\in = 1/n$ in the population n.

Definition 5.2 *Strategy $x \in \Delta$ is a strongly stable strategy when $\lim_{\bar{\in}_y \to 1} \in$ exists, which satisfies inequality 5.16 for every strategy $y \neq x$,*

$$E[x, y\lim_{\varepsilon \to 1}\varepsilon + (1 - \lim_{\varepsilon \to 1}\varepsilon)x] > E[y, y\lim_{\varepsilon \to 1}\varepsilon + (1 - \lim_{\varepsilon \to 1}\varepsilon)x]. \tag{5.16}$$

This definition describes that when a single original player who plays strategy x exists among the population, he or she retains his or her strategy because the payoff of this strategy is more than that of the strategy of any invader over interactions. Hence, even if the system becomes turbulent (all individuals play mutant strategy y), strategy x is also strongly stable, as shown in Figure 5.12(2).

Definition 5.3 *Strategy $x \in \Delta$ is an unstable strategy when $\lim_{\varepsilon \to 0} \in$ exists, which means that inequality 5.17 exists for every strategy $y \neq x$,*

$$E[x, y\lim_{\varepsilon \to 0}\varepsilon + (1 - \lim_{\varepsilon \to 0}\varepsilon)x] < E[y, y\lim_{\varepsilon \to 0}\varepsilon + (1 - \lim_{\varepsilon \to 0}\varepsilon)x]. \tag{5.17}$$

This definition implies that even if the single mutant strategy y appears in a large population, the remaining individuals that follow strategy x will change to strategy y by comparing the actual payoffs. Hence, even slight turbulence (a single invader) in the system makes strategy x unstable, as described in Figure 5.12(3).

Definition 5.4 *Strategy $x \in \Delta$ is a weakly stable strategy if there exists $\in (\lim_{\varepsilon \to 0} \in, \lim_{\varepsilon \to 1} \in)$ so that inequality 5.18 is met for every strategy $y \neq x$,*

$$E[x, \in y + (1 - \in)x] > E[y, \in y + (1 - \in)x]. \tag{5.18}$$

Compared with Definitions 5.2 and 5.3, this definition describes the situation when a low degree of turbulence (i.e., between $lim_{\varepsilon\to0}\in$ and $lim_{\varepsilon\to1}\in$ individuals that adopt mutant strategy y) emerges in the population involving someone with strategy x, namely that strategy x is weakly stable (see Figure 5.12(1)).

Proposition 5.1 *The trust strategy in barter exchange is an unstable strategy.*

Proof: If the *trust* strategy is *an unstable strategy*, then the condition in Definition 5.3 is satisfied. Without loss of generality, it can be assumed that in a large population, every individual randomly plays a symmetric game in barter exchange (for the interactive structure, see Figure 2.7), of which $\in$ frequencies of individuals as invaders play the *exploit* strategy and $(1-\in)$ individuals choose the *trust* strategy. The composition of population g is $(1-\in)$ *trust* $+ \in$ exploit. For individuals that play the trust strategy, the actual payoffs are given by:

$$E[trust,\in exploit+(1-\in)trust]=a(1-\in)+\in(-b).$$

For individuals that play the exploit strategy, the actual payoff is:

$$E[exploit,\in \exp loit+(1-\in)trust]=(a+x)(1-\in)+0\in.$$

From two equations, it is easy to show that:

$$E\,[trust,\in exploit+(1-\in)trust]-E[exploit,\in exploit+(1-\in)trust]$$

$$=a(1-\in)+\in(-b)-(a+x)(1-\in)-0\in=a-a\in-b\in-a-x+a\in+x\in$$

$$=(\in-1)x-b\in.$$

Note that for any $\in,x>0$, and $b>0,(\in-1)x-b\in<0$, so that:

$$E[trust,\in exploit+(1-\in)trust]<E[exploit,\in exploit+(1-\in)trust]$$

$$\to E[x,ylim_{\varepsilon\to0}\in+(1-lim_{\varepsilon\to0}\in)]x<E[x,ylim_{\varepsilon\to0}\in+(1-lim_{\varepsilon\to0}\in)x]$$

($\in$ is arbitrarily small).

Therefore, trust in barter exchange is an unstable strategy. Arbitrarily low turbulence (a single exploiter that adopts the exploit strategy emerges in the population) erodes the trust strategy.

ESSs in monetary and Internet exchanges: An asymmetric interactive structure

The above showed that the stability of trust in the barter economy is extraordinarily weak because of the barter system itself, meaning that slight turbulence (i.e., a single mutant in the population playing the trust strategy) leads to instability and the erosion of trusting behaviors. The evolution of economies has shifted interactive structures from symmetric to asymmetric ones (see section "Micro-to-macro transition of trust in exchange systems: Trust in different interactive structures and populations"). Hence, an asymmetric monetary system (e.g., asymmetric interactive structure) consequentially acts upon the behaviors of agents, thereby affecting the stability of trust in the interactive process. Indeed, according to Selten (1980), Maynard Smith (1982), and Cressman (1992), stability in asymmetric systems is particularly sensitive to the stability of the behaviors in the opposite group. Although this is different to the symmetric system, the basic rule of comparing the actual payoffs of the stability of behaviors remains in principle. Let us define the concepts of stability in the asymmetric context as a foundation for modeling the stability of trust in the following section.

Again, suppose that there are two groups in which individuals play an asymmetric game in a large interactive context. At the beginning, ε frequencies of mutant strategy $z \in \Delta$ and $(1 - \varepsilon)$ individuals playing strategy h exist in group A. Thus, if g_A is the profile distribution of group A, it is equal to $\varepsilon z + (1 - \varepsilon)h$, $\varepsilon \in (0,1)$. In the same vein, a θ ratio of a mutant strategy $j \in \Delta$ and a $(1 - \theta)$ proportion of agents with strategy k exist in group B. Note that these strategies do not play 2 X 2 games within the groups, but rather play intergroup, and that strategies can be better or worse off when encountering mutant strategies (see the matrixes in Figures 2.9 and 2.10). Similarly, the profile distribution $g_B = \theta j + (1-\theta)k$, $\theta \in (0,1)$. $E(z,g_B)$ and $E(h, g_B)$ are the functions of the actual payoffs of each individual playing strategies z and h, respectively encountering the profile distribution g_B, in a similar manner, for $E(j, g_A)$ and $E(k, g_A)$.

Definition 5.5(a) *Strategy $h \in \Delta$ is a double strongly stable strategy when $\theta \rightarrow 1$ and $\varepsilon \rightarrow 1$* (infinitely approaching one) *exist, which satisfies inequalities 5.19 (1) and (2) simultaneously for every strategy $h \neq z$ and $k \neq j$,*

(1) $E[h, j\theta + (1-\theta)k] > E[z, j\theta + (1-\theta)k]$,

(2) $E[k, z\varepsilon + (1-\varepsilon)h] > E[j, z\varepsilon + (1-\varepsilon)h]$. $\quad$ (5.19)

This definition means that when the greatest turbulence (mutant strategies z and j) simultaneously appears in the two groups, both original strategies are stable because of the payoffs from the interactions.

Definition 5.5(b) *Strategy $h \in \Delta$ is a single strongly stable strategy when* $\theta \rightarrow$ *1and* $\varepsilon \rightarrow$ *1* (infinitely approaching one), *which satisfies inequalities 5.20(1) and (2) simultaneously for every strategy $h \pm z$ and $k \neq j$,*

$$(1)\quad E[h, j\theta + (1-\theta)k] > E[z, j\theta + (1-\theta)k],$$
$$(2)\quad E[k, z\varepsilon + (1-\varepsilon)h] < E[j, z\varepsilon + (1-\varepsilon)h]. \tag{5.20}$$

Definition 5.6(a) *Strategy $h \in \Delta$ is a double unstable strategy when* $\theta \rightarrow 0$ *and* $\varepsilon \rightarrow 0$, *which satisfies two inequalities 5.21(1) and (2) or every strategy $h \neq z$ and $k \neq j$,*

$$(1)\quad E[h, j\theta + (1-\theta)k] < E[z, j\theta + (1-\theta)k]$$
$$(2)\quad E[k, z\varepsilon + (1-\varepsilon)h] < E[j, z\varepsilon + (1-\varepsilon)h]. \tag{5.21}$$

This definition suggests that when a slight turbulence (single mutant strategies z and j) appears in both groups, they shift their original strategies to a mutant one, which is extremely unstable.

Definition 5.6(b) *Strategy $h \in \Delta$ is a single unstable strategy when* $\theta \rightarrow 0$ *and* $\varepsilon \rightarrow 0$, *which satisfies two inequalities 5.21(1) and (2) for every strategy $h \neq z$ and $k \neq j$,*

$$(1)\quad E[h, j\theta + (1-\theta)k] < E[z, j\theta + (1-\theta)k]$$
$$(2)\quad E[k, z\varepsilon + (1-\varepsilon)h] > E[j, z\varepsilon + (1-\varepsilon)h]. \tag{5.22}$$

Definition 5.7(a) *Strategy $h \in \Delta$ is a double weakly stable strategy when* $\theta \in (\theta \rightarrow 0, \theta \rightarrow 1)$ *and* $\varepsilon \in (\varepsilon \rightarrow 0, \varepsilon \rightarrow 1)$, *which satisfies two inequalities 5.23(1) and (2) for every strategy $h \neq z$ and $k \neq j$,*

$$(1)\quad E[h, j\theta + (1-\theta)k] > E[z, j\theta + (1-\theta)k]$$
$$(2)\quad E[k, z\varepsilon + (1-\varepsilon)h] > E[j, z\varepsilon + (1-\varepsilon)h]. \tag{5.23}$$

Definition 5.7(b) *Strategy $h \in \Delta$ is a single weakly stable strategy when* $\theta \in (\theta \rightarrow 0, \theta \rightarrow 1)$ *and* $\varepsilon \in (\varepsilon \rightarrow 0, \varepsilon \rightarrow 1)$ *which satisfies inequalities 5.24(1) and (2) for every strategy $h \neq z$ and $k \neq j$,*

$$(1)\quad E[h, j\theta + (1-\theta)k] > E[z, j\theta + (1-\theta)k]$$
$$(2)\quad E[k, z\varepsilon + (1-\varepsilon)h] < E[j, z\varepsilon + (1-\varepsilon)h]. \tag{5.24}$$

Proposition 5.2 *The trust strategy in monetary exchange is a single weakly stable strategy.*

Proof: Suppose group A is the *buyer* group and group B the *seller* group in which individuals play asymmetric games in a largely random interaction. The asymmetric interactive structure is shown in Figure 2.9. At the beginning, in the *buyer* group ε individuals follow the mutant strategy (*distrust*) and $(1 - \varepsilon)$ play the *trust* strategy. Similarly, in the *seller* group, θ agents play the mutant strategy (*exploit*) and $(1 - \theta)$ the *honor* strategy. Suppose:

$$F_1 = E[\text{trust}, \text{exploit}\,\theta + (1-\theta)\text{honor}] -$$
$$E[\text{distrust}, \text{exploit}\,\theta + (1-\theta)\,\text{honor}], \text{and}$$
$$F_2 = E[\text{honor}, \text{distrust}\,\varepsilon + (1-\varepsilon)\,\text{trust}] -$$
$$E[\text{exploit}, \text{distrust}\,\varepsilon + (1-\varepsilon)\,\text{trust}].$$

On the basis of the interactive structure of the monetary system, it can be generalized that:

$$F_1 = a(1-\theta) - b\theta - 0(1-\theta) + 0\theta$$
$$= a - (a+b)\theta.$$

For $0 < b < a$, if $\theta \to 0$, there exists $F_1 > 0$; if $\theta \to 1$, there is $F_1 < 0$; if $\theta = a/(a+b)$, there is $F_1 = 0$. Moreover, since $(dF_1)/d\theta > 0$, $\theta \in [\theta \to 0, a/(a+b))$, making $F_1 > 0$ and $\theta \in (a/(a+b), \theta \to 1]$, resulting in $F_1 < 0$. Similarly, let us consider equation F_2 as follows:

$$F_2 = a(1-\varepsilon) - f\varepsilon - (a+x)(1-\varepsilon)$$
$$= (x-f)\varepsilon - x.$$

For $0 < f < x$, if $\varepsilon \to 0$, $F_2 < 0$; if $\varepsilon \to 1$, $F_2 < 0$. Because $(dF_2)/d\varepsilon > 0$, $\varepsilon \in [\varepsilon \to 0, \varepsilon \to 1]$, $F_2 < 0$. By combining the parameters θ and ε, it can be referenced that when $\theta \in [\theta \to 0, a/(a+b)]$, $\varepsilon \in [\varepsilon \to 0, \varepsilon \to 1]$, $F_1 > 0$ and $F_2 < 0$, meaning so that according to Definition 5.7(b), trust is a single weakly stable strategy.

Proposition 5.3 *The trust strategy in Internet exchange is a double weakly stable strategy when $(x - m) < 0$.*

Proof: Internet exchange is different from monetary exchange because it includes the enforcement of third parties, which creates underlying losses m for individuals who play the *exploit* strategy. The interactive structure is shown in Figure 2.11. Based on this, together with the same treatments as Proposition 5.2, we can see that the outcomes of equation F_1 in the Internet system are the same as those in the monetary system. Therefore, here we can directly consider F_2. According to the interactive structure in Figure 2.10:

$$F_2 = a(1-\varepsilon) - f\varepsilon - (a+x-m)(1-\varepsilon)$$
$$= (x-m-f)\varepsilon - x + m.$$

Assuming $F_2 > 0$, it can be obtained that:

$$(x - m - f)\varepsilon - x + m > 0.$$

1   As $(x - m - f) > 0, \varepsilon > \dfrac{x - m}{x - f - m}$ (but $\dfrac{x - m}{x - f - m} > 1$, so it is deleted).

2(1)   As $(x - m - f) < 0$ and $(x - m) < 0, \varepsilon < \dfrac{m - x}{m - x + f} \in (0, \ 1)$.

(2)   As $(x - m - f) < 0$ and $(x - m) > 0$, $\varepsilon < 0$ (it is deleted).

Hence, $\varepsilon \in (\varepsilon \to 0, \varepsilon \to 1)$ and when $(x - m) < 0, F_2 > 0$ can be satisfied. Together with the results of F_1 (in Proposition 5.2), the trust strategy is a double weakly stable strategy when $(x - m) < 0$. Of course, by setting $F_2 < 0$, when $(x - f - m) > 0$ and $(x - m) > 0, F_2 < 0$. Therefore, under this condition the trust strategy in Internet exchange is a single weakly stable strategy.

The stability analysis of trust in exchange systems: A dynamic prediction

The above discussion suggested that the stability of trust is more likely to be decided by the exchange systems themselves, by comparing the payoffs between the original and intrusive behavioral types of individuals collected over all interactions. This approach is a useful means to explain the stability of systems in a static prediction. In this section, I follow the general setting that exchange systems are assumed to be dynamic, namely that the number of individuals with different behaviors (i.e., strategies) varies over time. This interpretation reflects the process of birth and death in a large population and considers the stability of trust from two aspects: how trust is stable in dynamic processes and the characteristics of stability.

In the section "Micro-to-macro transition of trust in exchange systems: Trust in different interactive structures and populations," models of the evolution of trust developed by using replicator dynamics in exchange systems were presented. However, because trust moves to generate the processes of birth and death in a large population over time, these models cannot explain the stability of trust, where the stability points are, or how strong they could be. Explicitly, I thus refer to these equations of replicator dynamics in order to explore the stability of trust in dynamic exchange systems. To define and analyze the stability of trust in dynamic systems, the stable strategy (Maynard Smith and Price, 1973; Selten, 1980) dealt with in replicator dynamics is used. Before we go into the detail, however, this concept should be simply introduced.

Stable states

The earliest empirical reflection of SSs was provided by Taylor and Jonker (1978), who changed the concept of ESS into a dynamic one by insisting that "individuals tend to switch to strategies that are doing well, or that individuals bear offspring who tend to use the same strategies as their parent" (p. 146). To improve this idea, they first provided a concept of population states, indicating frequencies of individuals with the same strategy. This concept was then placed into a differential equation to represent its changes in number over time. This equation is now called a replicator equation, which comprises the population state of individuals with the same strategy and growth rate (i.e., fitness):

$$\dot{m} = m(\pi_i^{Trust} - \pi^{Average}).$$

The replicator equation emphasizes the following process. If an individual's payoff is higher than the population average, the number of the types of behaviors he or she displays (population state) will increase over time proportional to the outcomes in value of subtracting individual payoffs from average payoffs, in line with the view of Taylor and Jonker (1978). Simple logic can help us understand the stability of this system when the replicator equation is equal to zero, i.e. the change stops. In such a condition, these population states are called SSs.

From a mathematical perspective, the replicator equation as a differential linear model may have several stable points equal to zero. In particular, these may be the final outcomes of this dynamic system, although their function uniformly satisfies this formula. Based on a general treatment, we must distinguish whether these population states are a final result of a system evolving (i.e., final SS). In this part, I use the following cases on the stability of trust in a specific analysis to provide an explanation.

Stability of trust in dynamic barter exchange

The basic thinking behind replicator dynamics is that "good" behavior (i.e., strategy) increases gradually or rapidly over time and, ultimately, that this is accepted by more interacting individuals. To elaborate on this phenomenon in barter exchange, reconsider the replicator equation of trust in the barter economy:

$$\dot{m} = m(1 - m)\,[(b - x)m - b]. \tag{5.4}$$

In this equation, m ($m \leq 1$) represents the population state of individuals that follow a trust strategy. Although the change in this population state over time was explained in the section "Micro-to-macro transition of trust in

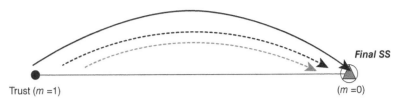

Trust ($m = 1$)   ($m = 0$)

Figure 5.13 The stability of trust in dynamic barter exchange. The dashed arrow
signifies the direction of evolution.

exchange systems: Trust in different interactive structures and populations,"
where this system will evolve into stability has not yet been emphasized.
In other words, what is the SS of trust in this dynamic barter system? Let
equation (5.4) equal zero in order to yield the following two SSs:

$$m = 0, m = 1, \left(\text{not } m = \frac{b}{b-x},\right.$$

because $\dfrac{b}{b-x} > 1$, for $b > x > 0$), respectively.

In a similar way, the criteria for the judgment of the final SS in a symmetric
replicator dynamic system from Nowak and Sigmund (1998) are applied
here. According to these criteria, if strategy A dominates strategy B in the
interactive structure, population state A will be the final SS and the dynamic
system will converge toward that point. Hence, the exploit strategy dominates the trust strategy in barter exchange (see Figure 2.7, where $a + x > a$ and
$0 > (-b)$), meaning that $m = 0$ is the final SS. This finding suggests that the
population state of trust will evolve from any initial point to zero because
the system is in a dynamic process (see Figures 5.9 and 5.13).

Stability of trust in dynamic monetary exchange

In this part, I interpret the stability of trust embedded in double replicator equations, encountering a dynamic asymmetric interactive process
in monetary exchange. This time, the question is whether the stability of
trust is dependent on the stability of other matters in another replicator
dynamic. From a theoretical perspective, this is understood as an issue
of the stability of two dynamic systems in an asymptotic process. In this
context, Selten (1980), Cressman (1992), and Weibull (1995) all provided
a common rule for analyzing this issue by assessing a *Jacobian Matrix*.
In this study, this rule is considered in the case of the stability of trust in
dynamic monetary exchange.

The replicator dynamic equations of the evolution of trust in monetary exchange were discussed in section "Replicator dynamics of trust in a heterogeneous population: Monetary exchange," which showed that the replicator dynamic equation of trust in the buyer group is given by:

$$\dot{n} = n(1-n)[(a+b)l - b]. \tag{5.8}$$

Similarly, the replicator dynamic equation of honor in the seller group is:

$$\dot{i} = l(1-l)[(f-x)n - f]. \tag{5.9}$$

Let $\dot{n} = 0$ and $\dot{i} = 0$, which provides four SSs by combining the points in each replicator model: $(0,0), (0,1), (1,0),$ and $(1,1)$ (not $(\dfrac{f}{f-x}, \dfrac{b}{a+b})$), $\dfrac{f}{f-x} < 0$, for $f < x$). Then, these points are checked by using a *Jacobian Matrix* to assess whether the SSs are final stable points. According to the two replicator dynamic equations, the *Jacobian Matrix* can be calculated as follows:

$$J = \begin{pmatrix} (1-2n)[(a+b) \, l - b] & n(1-n)(a+b) \\ l(1-l)(f-x) & (1-2l)[(f-x)n - f] \end{pmatrix}.$$

Based on the criteria provided by Selten (1980), Cressman (1992), and Weibull (1995), when the points simultaneously satisfy the two conditions $det(J) > 0$ and $tr(J) < 0$, they are final SSs (Figure 5.14). The calculative outcomes are presented in Table 5.2.

Stability of trust in dynamic Internet exchange

As shown earlier, the stability of trust in dynamic Internet exchange within an asymmetric interactive structure includes enforcement by third parties (see Figure 2.10). Under such circumstances, intuitively, and perhaps logically, the characteristics of the stability of trust are affected by this enforcement. However, we must carefully examine how and where final SSs are reached, despite the similarity of the treatment with dynamic monetary exchange. Hence, I return to the replicator equations of the evolution of trust in Internet exchange (see section "Replicator dynamics of trust in a

Table 5.2 Outcomes of the stability of trust in dynamic monetary exchange

Points	Det (J)	Tr (J)	Outcome
(0, 0)	+	−	SS
(1, 1)	−	−	Saddle point
(0, 1)	+	+	Unstable
(1, 0)	−	+	Saddle point

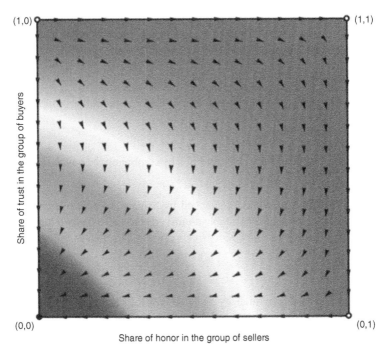

Figure 5.14 Stability of trust in monetary exchange. The arrows signify the direction of evolution.

Source: Created by Dynamo (Sandholm *et al.*, 2012).

heterogeneous population with enforcements: Internet exchange"). Here, the replicator equation of the evolution of trust in the buyer group is given by:

$$\dot{g} = g(1-g)\big[(a+b)k - b\big], \tag{5.13}$$

and the replicator equation of the evolution of honor in the seller group is characterized by:

$$\dot{k} = k(1-k)\big[(m+f-x)g - f\big]. \tag{5.14}$$

Equations (5.13) and (5.14) yield five population states: $(0,0), (0,1), (1,0), 1, 1)$, and $(\dfrac{f}{m+f-x}, \dfrac{b}{a+b})$. Before discussing the final SSs with these popula-tion states, however, it is noted that the fifth one (i.e., $(\dfrac{f}{m+f-x}, \dfrac{b}{a+b})$) is required to classify two situations because of enforcement *m* (for a simple

Table 5.3 Outcomes of the stability of trust in Internet exchange

Points	Det (J)	Tr (J)	Outcome
(0, 0)	+	−	SS
(1, 1)	−	unknown	Saddle point ($m < x$)
	+	−	SS ($m > x$)
(0, 1)	+	+	Unstable point
(1, 0)	−	unknown	Saddle point ($m < x$)
	+	+	Unstable point ($m > x$)
($f/(m + f−x)$, $b/(a + b)$)	+	0	Saddle point

discussion of this issue, see section "Replicator dynamics of trust in a heterogeneous population with enforcements: Internet exchange"):

1 When $m + f - x < 0$, the point $(\dfrac{f}{m + f - x}, \dfrac{b}{a+b})$ does not exist. The analytical outcomes for the final SSs of trust in Internet exchange are the same as those in dynamic monetary exchange. This finding implies that underlying enforcement m is ineffective at preventing exploitation by sellers because the payoffs that arise from defection (x) are more than those brought about by enforcement (m).

2 When $m + f - x > 0$, the point $(\dfrac{f}{m + f - x}, \dfrac{b}{a+b})$ exists. Then, we can obtain the *Jacobian Matrix* as follows:

$$J = \begin{pmatrix} (1-2g)[(a+b)\,k-b] & g(1-g)(a+b) \\ k(1-k)(m+f-x) & (1-2k)\,[(m+f-x)g-f] \end{pmatrix}.$$

According to the same criteria as monetary exchange, the outcomes are presented in Table 5.3.

Based on these conditions, we can design two pictures of the outcomes of the stability of trust in this system (see Figures 5.15 and 5.16).

Summary

The micro-to-macro transition of trust is affected by the different matching rules and populations that arise in distinct economies such as barter and monetary exchanges (section "Micro-to-macro transition of trust in exchange systems: Trust in different interactive structures and populations"). By using EGT and applying replicator dynamics, different phenomena of the micro-to-macro transition of trust were shown. In particular, the evolution of trust in barter exchange is characterized by a decreased and linear trajectory over

(1,0)   (1,1)

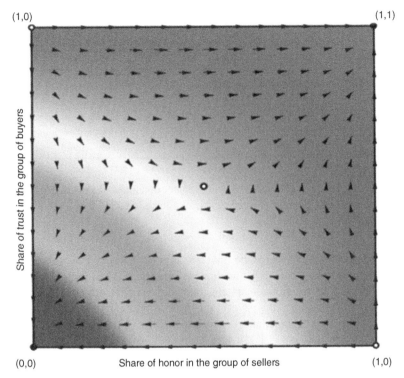

(0,0)   Share of honor in the group of sellers   (1,0)

Figure 5.15 The stability of trust in Internet exchange ($m > x$).

Source: Created by Dynamo (Sandholm *et al.*, 2012).

time, in monetary exchange by an increase or decrease dependent on the initial conditions (i.e., the number of agents with honor), and in Internet exchange by various trends. These findings explain that barter exchange does not support the evolution of trust, whereas monetary and Internet exchanges allow trust to flourish under certain conditions. This result sheds light on the evolution of trust in barter and monetary economies introduced in section "The phenomena of the co-evolution of trust and exchange systems: Trust in barter and monetary economies."

In addition, exchange systems influence the stability of trust in static and dynamic predictions (section "Stability of trust"). When the concept of ESS is introduced in a static consideration, trust is proven to be an unstable strategy in barter exchange, a single weakly stable strategy in monetary exchange, and a double weakly stable strategy in Internet exchange. Further, when the concept of SS is dynamic, trust is not verified as an SS

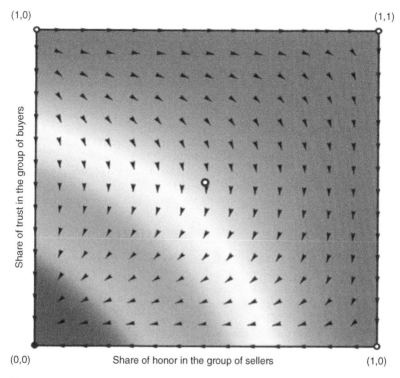

Figure 5.16 The stability of trust in Internet exchange ($x - f < m < x$).

Source: Created by Dynamo (Sandholm *et al.*, 2012).

in dynamic barter or monetary exchanges, but as an SS in dynamic Internet exchange when $m > x$. Therefore, a general theory of the collective stability of trust in large transition economies is concluded. This theory suggests that exchange systems sustain different levels of stability of trust. In the next chapter, we further discuss the varieties of changes in trust when the dynamic process of trust is affected by turbulence, which can be used as a metaphor for real-life interactions.

References

Bendor, J., Swistak, P. 1997. The Evolutionary Stability of Cooperation. *American Political Science Review*, 91(2), 290–307.
Coleman, J.S. 1990. *Foundations of Social Theory*. Cambridge, MA: Harvard University Press.

Cressman, R. 1992. *The Stability Concept of Evolutionary Game Theory: A Dynamic Approach.* Berlin: Springer-Verlag.

Dasgupta, P. 2000. Trust as a Commodity. In: Gambetta, D. (Ed.), *Trust: Making and Breaking Cooperative Relation.* Oxford: University of Oxford, 49–72.

European Bank for Reconstruction and Development 1999. *Transition Report.* London: EBRD, 26–27.

Gaunersdorfer, A., Hofbauer, J., Sigmund, K. 1991. On the Dynamics of Asymmetric Games. *Theoretical Population Biology*, 39, 345–357.

Johnson, S., Kaufmann, D., Shleifer, A. 1997. The Unofficial Economy in Transition. *Brookings Papers on Economic Activity*, 2, 159–239.

Knack, S., Philip, K. 1997. Does Social Capital have a Payoff? A Cross-Country Investigation. *Quarterly Journal of Economics*, 112(4), 1251–1288.

Maynard Smith, J. 1974. The Theory of Games and Evolution of Animal Conflicts. *Journal of Theoretical Biology*, 47, 209–221.

Maynard Smith, J. 1982. *Evolution and the Theory of Games.* Cambridge, UK: Cambridge University Press.

Maynard Smith, J., Price, G.R. 1973. The Logic of Animal Conflict. *Nature*, 246, 15–18.

Nowak, M., Sigmund, K. 1998. The Dynamics of Indirect Reciprocity. *Journal of Theoretical Biology*, 194, 561–574.

Sandholm, W.H., Dokumaci, E., Franchetti, F. 2012. *Dynamo: Diagrams for Evolutionary Game Dynamics.* Available at: http://www.ssc.wisc.edu/~whs/dynamo (accessed 10 March 2014).

Santos, F.C., Pacheco, J.M., Lenaerts, T. 2006. Evolutionary Dynamics of Social Dilemmas in Structured Heterogeneous Populations. *PNAS*, 103(9), 3490–3494.

Schelling, T.C. 1960. *The Strategy of Conflict.* New York, NY: Oxford University Press.

Selten, R. 1980. A Note on Evolutionary Stable Strategies in Asymmetric Contests. *Journal of Theoretical Biology*, 84, 93–101.

Simmel, G. 1990. *The Philosophy of Money.* 2nd edition. London: Routledge. Translated from the 1907 German edition by Tom Bottomore and David Frisby [Original ed. 1900.] .

Skaggs, N.T. 1998. Debt as the Basis of Currency: The Monetary Economic of Trust. *American Journal of Economics and Sociology*, 57(4), 453–467.

Smith, A. 1776. *An Inquiry into the Nature and Causes of the Wealth of Nations.* Oxford: Oxford University Press.

Taylor, P., Jonker, L. 1978. Evolutionary Stable Strategies and Game Dynamics. *Mathematical Biosciences*, 40, 145–156.

Weibull, J.W. 1995. *Evolutionary Game Theory.* London: MIT Press.

Weibull, J.W. 1998. What Have we Learned from Evolutionary Game Theory so far? Research Institute of Industrial Economics. Working Papers 487, Research Institute of Industrial Economics. Available at: http://ideas.repec.org/p/hhs/iuiwop/0487.html (accessed 30 May 2015).

Young, H.P. 1998. *Individual Strategy and Social Structure: An Evolutionary Theory of Institutions.* Princeton, NJ: Princeton University Press.

6 Varieties of trust

Economic trends have influenced the evolution and stability of trust, especially when trust is considered to be an embedded exchange process. In the last chapter, replicator equations were used to show a series of interactive trust phenomena with respect to exchange systems (e.g., the evolution of trust in barter, monetary, and Internet exchanges). In this chapter, I consider a particular fact of the dynamic transactional process: interaction often generates "noises" (Nowak *et al.*, 2004). The dynamic process of trust in exchange systems may be forced by many types of noises such as immigration, spatial structures, and institutions, producing a time lag to the interaction that affects evolutionary processes and results in dynamic changes that rest on these noises. Hence, this chapter considers this context to explain the dynamic process of trust in general interactions.

The body of research on how the evolution process is influenced by noise in a dynamic system (e.g., a replicator dynamic system) includes the works of Foster and Young (1990), Freidlin and Wentzell (1994), and Young (1998). These studies viewed the impact of noises as creating a Gaussian white noise in the dynamic system. However, by integrating all noises into one factor, these authors failed to point out how a concrete factor (e.g., spatial structure) acts upon the dynamic processes. Further, they did not offer a reasonable and specific interpretation of the bifurcations in the dynamic processes of a system.

In this chapter, therefore, I focus on bridging this gap by examining one function of a structured interaction, namely the overlap between an interaction network and a learning network on the evolution of trust in dynamic barter exchange. The aim here is to enhance our understanding of the relationship between the bifurcation of the evolution of trust and noise, further explaining why varieties of trust exist in this process.

To meet this purpose, I first consider varieties of changes in trust in light of the evolutionary theories of stochastic dynamics, especially the theory of

Foster and Young (1990), discussing how all noises influence the dynamic process of trust over time. Then, the overlap between an interaction network and a learning network is analyzed in detail in order to explain these varieties of changes in trust.

Theory of stochastic dynamics in Foster and Young (1990): Implication for varieties of changes in trust

An obvious weakness of replicator dynamics and the other evolutionary dynamics mentioned throughout this book is that the interpretation of evolutionarily dynamic behaviors (i.e., strategies) emphasizes the advantage of a behavior itself – a dominant behavior is assumed to increase more rapidly than a dominated one over time – and places less stress on how small perturbations affect dynamic processes.

Foster and Young (1990) directly considered noises in replicator dynamics and demonstrated, fundamentally and clearly, that even if arbitrarily small stochastic noises are created for various reasons, these cumulatively influence the evolution process, finally altering the long-run dynamic process in a system. According to Foster and Young's (1990) theory, noises inevitably occur both in the game itself (e.g., the variability of payoffs depending on the environment) and in the time delay for individuals to interact. Hence, there is reason to believe that the dynamic process of trust in exchange systems also suffers from these issues and that trust changes over time under the continual and isolated influence of noises. Let us turn to this point through the example of the replicator dynamics of trust in the barter system with noises.

Trust with noise: Example of varieties of changes in trust in barter exchange

As an example, let us start with a replicator dynamic model of the evolution of trust in barter exchange (see equation (5.4), repeated below). Micro-level trusting behavior in dynamic barter exchange in an interactive structure such as PD is converted into the state of trust in the system. Under such a circumstances, trust decreases continually over time before eroding entirely (see Figure 5.9). However, the presented analysis emphasizes how the barter system itself affects the dynamic process of trust over time and less how this system influences trust when noises are inevitably involved.

In fact, in barter exchange noise is created from various sources. For example, individuals might not barter continuously, while social norms, institutions, morals, and other things could also influence individual behavior in the exchange process. These points suggest that exchange is filled with noises as well as influencing the dynamic process of trust over time:

$$\dot{m} = m(t)\,(1 - m(t))\,\big[(b - x)m(t) - b\big].\tag{5.4}$$

Given the effect of the noise involved, "assuming that the population and the number of interactions per period are large, these sources of variability can be well-approximated by a continuous-time, continuous space Wiener process" (Foster and Young, 1990, p. 6). In this way, equation (5.4) can be rewritten as:

$$dm(t)/dt = m(t)\,(1 - m(t))\,\big[(b - x)m(t) - b\big] + \sigma dW(t)/dt,\tag{6.1}$$

where $W(t) \sim N(0, t)$ and σ is the intensity of noise. This equation shows that the noise factor $W(t)$ will continuously run into the replicator equation over time, while σ ($0 \leq \sigma \leq 1$) is a weight factor that controls for the strength of this effect in each time step. Hence, when σ is increased, noise accumulates rapidly over time, and when σ is decreased, this aggregated dynamic process slows. The factor σ may influence the evolution of trust in the barter economy provided noise exists. Following this idea, simulating equation (6.1) helps us envisage the function of σ (see Figure 6.1).

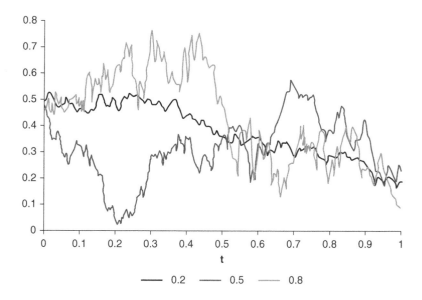

Figure 6.1 Varieties of change in trust in a barter economy. Parameters: $b = 0.6$, $x = 0.4$, m (initial value) $= 0.5$, step size $= 0.05$, and $\sigma = 0.2, 0.5, 0.8$.

Figure 6.1 illustrates that the simulated dynamic process of trust varies in response to different values of σ. At $\sigma = 0.2$ or lower, for example, the path of the dynamic process of trust over time is similar to that in Figure 5.9, i.e. trust decreases. By contrast, at $\sigma = 0.5$ and 0.8 or being arbitrarily larger, changes in trust fluctuate.

A further conclusion thus is that noise may affect dynamic changes in trust – sometimes in a destructive orientation and sometimes in the reverse direction – contingent on their strength (i.e., σ in this context). This conclusion allows us to explain the varieties of changes in trust in reality, as explored further in the following section. Nevertheless, it is not enough to consider a comprehensive noise by simply examining the varieties of changes in trust using a simple mathematical method. Similarly, it is not sufficient to find out how a concrete noise affects the dynamic process in reality or assume that the rule exists at the micro level, while chaotic phenomena spread at the macro level. This approach would suggest that the presented model does not approximate reality in general.

Trust in overlapping networks: Noise and varieties of change

Foster and Young (1990) stated the importance of recognizing exactly how noise as a whole exists, assuming that noise is treated as a noise parameter following a random process. This enhances our understanding of the cause of varieties of phenomena in a dynamic system, which is referred to as the "intensity of noise" in a Wiener process. However, we do not simply say that reality is filled with noise; rather, we aim to find out how noise is produced and how it affects the dynamic processes of phenomena. In this section, I examine the noise created by structured interactions in reality, which affect the dynamic process of trust and lead to varieties of changes in trust.

Previous authors have already focused on the issue of the *evolution of trust in networks* (e.g., Gintis, 2000; Güth and Kliemt, 2004; Hardin, 2006). Nevertheless, the present study is the first to consider the impact of overlapping networks on the evolution of trust in order to explain varieties of changes in trust because of structured interactions.

Each individual forms relationships and plays games with his or her neighbors in an interaction network that is stable over time. Hence, the individual learns or imitates the behaviors of members, which leads to the formation of a so-called replacement (learning) network that is dynamic over time (Suzuki and Arita, 2009) (see Figure 6.2). Most previous studies assume that both coincide, namely people just learn strategies (e.g., behaviors) from their interaction network members. Breaking the symmetry between them aims to emphasize the fact that decisions on actions are dependent

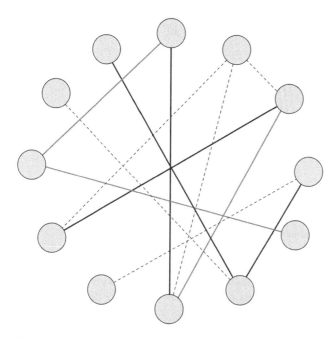

Figure 6.2 Overlapping networks.

Note: points are agents. The networks with dotted lines are learning networks and the networks with gray lines are interaction networks. The black lines combined with dotted and gray are the overlapping parts of both networks.

not only on the behaviors of their neighbors in the interactions but also on the information about other individual behaviors in the networks. Thus, we distinguish relationships in the learning network from those in the interaction network. For example, in the real world, people can earn payoffs, learn skills, and ascertain knowledge from network partners as well as simultaneously obtaining identical things from others outside the network.

The overlapping structure between two networks creates a structured interaction that applies to the general situation of interactions assumed to exist in the context of evolution, namely a large randomly interacting population. This turbulence, in which people interact with their neighbors, from the interaction network as a routine, and learning from members in the learning network provides a particularly structured setting for the study of the evolution of trust in exchange.

The analysis above implies that the interaction network in both the social and the biological worlds is often scale-free and stable (see Figure 6.3), because some people have more neighbors than others (the main characteristic of

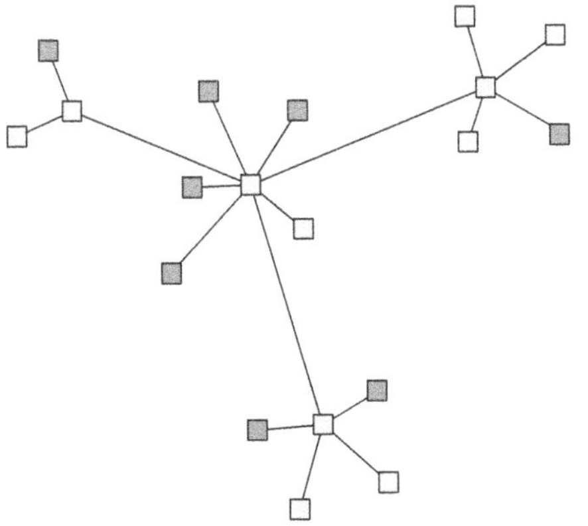

Figure 6.3 Scale-free networks.

a scale-free network) and a learning network is often dynamic because of the information flow on which agents base their decisions. In this section, I explore whether this structured interaction in both networks can bring about various changes in trust and under what conditions.

The model of overlapping networks and varieties of change in trust: Noise and self-organization phenomena

The "market" as a network to support the evolution of trust is a metaphor used in many trust studies. Nevertheless, it is often improperly understood as a single network. For example, Emerson (1978) and Hardin (2001), among other scholars, argued that trust evolves in a single network ("market") in which evolution is contingent on the network evolving. In essence, however, a market is not a single network but an overlapping one.

A common phenomenon in reality allows us to explore this overlapping network. First, rational individuals often form various stable relationships as a premise of exchange (e.g., circle of friends), as the exchange process permeates risks under uncertainty. Once these exchange relationships stabilize, the whole market can be imagined as a stable (interaction) network that aims to provide payoffs. Under such a circumstance, rational individuals must imitate their well-performing neighbors or learn the high-performing behaviors of individuals outside their pre-existing relationships through information floating in the network. Such a network formed by individuals learning from either their neighbors or outsiders is called a learning network. Therefore, a market exists for the evolution of behaviors in the form of overlapping networks provided dynamic learning processes are considered and exchange relationships stable.

According to this idea, I provide an overlapping model in which various changes in trust in appearance depend on the degree of overlap between both networks in order to explain the dynamic bifurcation of trust and show a self-organizing "market for trust."

A model of overlapping networks

In the model presented in this study, the interaction network is defined as a scale-free network, similar to that formulated by Barabási and Albert's (1999) model (see Figure 6.4). At the beginning of evolution, trustors and exploiters are equally and randomly distributed. They struggle to live by playing games with their neighbors and receive aggregate payoffs from interactions in each step of the evolutionary process. The interaction network is static in the evolutionary process, similar to the situation of employees signing long-term working contracts with employers or companies keeping stable relationships with partners in the long run. To model the learning network (replacement network), learning processes are included according to the observation that individuals learn from both neighbors and outsiders (although the proportion between these modes of learning differs over time).

Figure 6.4 Interaction networks. The number of agents is 1,000 and average connectivity is 2. This was created according to the preference attachment in Barabási and Albert's (1999) model and the algorithm of Wilensky (2005).

To describe this process, for every player, we set the probability of learning from a neighbor as p in each time step and that of learning from outsiders as $(1 - p)$. Based on this probability, when one player chooses a learning strategy, a link will be created. Likewise, if he or she chooses another learning strategy, this link will be deleted and rewired with the new one. Hence, the learning network differs over time to the extent that it dynamically overlaps with the interaction network. In particular, when $p = 0$, all players only learn from outsiders, indicating that neither network coincides (i.e., there are no links). By contrast, when $p = 1$, all players learn strategies from their neighbors in the interaction network, suggesting dynamic overlapping between both networks. When, for example, $p = 0.3$, players learn less often from their neighbors in the interaction network and more often from outsiders (in some sense, the degree of overlap is lower in each time step). Finally, when $p = 0.7$, agents more often learn from neighbors and less often from outsiders, meaning that the overlap is great.

For $p = 0.3$ and $p = 0.7$, I use the overlapping model above to generate an overlapping network (i.e., combination of interaction and learning networks) to show how the degree of overlap depends on probability p (see Figure 6.5). Figure 6.5(1) demonstrates that when $p = 0.3$, there are three overlapping links between the two networks (links with combined red and blue), while when $p = 0.7$, there are eight overlapping links (see Figure 6.5(2)). Hence, different degrees of overlap are created based on probability p, which provides a series of treatments to study how these structured settings affect the evolution of trust and further result in varieties of dynamic changes in trust.

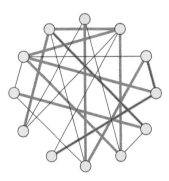

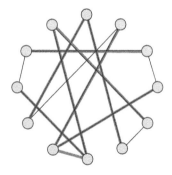

1. Learning networks generated
with $p = 0.3$

1. Learning networks generated
with $p = 0.7$

Figure 6.5 Overlapping networks (this study). The interaction network consists of gray links, while the learning network has black links. The solid lines mixing gray and black show the overlap between both networks. The average degree of the interaction network is 12, and this is a static random graph.

Source: Zhang (2004).

Strategy updating rules

Evolution is carried out in a finite population similar to that under replicator dynamics (i.e., imitation dynamics) (Gintis, 2000; Hauert and Doebeli, 2004; Santos *et al.*, 2006; see also Chapter 3, section "Basic concepts"). The interactive game is considered to be barter exchange (see Figure 2.7). The strategy updating rules are thus described as follows:

1 In each time step, each individual plays a game with his or her connected neighbors in the interaction network, with the sum of overall payoffs from interactions and their accumulated payoffs x_i, $i \in [1, 2, 3, \ldots, N]$.

2 Simultaneously, according to the overlapping model proposed herein, individuals select a neighbor or outsider from which to learn their strategies based on probability p. Those chosen are defined as partner A, whose payoff is labeled x_a.

3 If $x_a > x_i$, the strategy of partner A replaces that of individual i with a transition probability given by:

$$Z = (x_a - x_i) / [k \times (max(a + x, a) - min(-b, 0)], \qquad (6.2)$$

where $k = max(k_i, k_a)$, k_i is the number of individual i's neighbors and k_a the number of agent A's neighbors in the interaction network. In addition, $(a + x)$, a, $(-b)$ come from the interactive structure in the barter economy (see Figure 2.7).

4 The strategy updating process is synchronous for all individuals.

Simulations and results

We simulate the evolutionary process of trust in the barter economy in different overlapping models: $p = 0$, $p = 0.3$, $p = 0.7$, and $p = 1$. Experiments are performed on the interaction network (see Figure 6.4) of the initial population size $N = 1,000$ and average degree $d = 2$. At the beginning, equal percentages of individuals follow trust and exploit strategies, and these are randomly distributed in the interaction network. As the overlapping model shows, the interaction network is stable throughout evolution, while the learning network generated by probability p is changing.

What kind of aggregate behavior appears when individuals have different strategies under overlapping networks? The structure of partly overlapping networks may favor the evolution of trust, full of diversified and robust trust. The outcomes of the simulation confirm our expectations, but also provide special phenomena that we have not captured.

Figure 6.6 shows the frequency of trusting in the barter economy through the 1,400 steps of trials in the four cases of $p = 0, 0.3, 0.7$, and 1. This figure

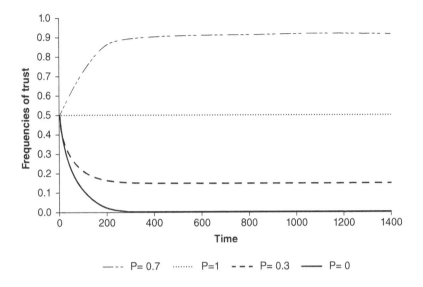

Figure 6.6 The effect of dynamically overlapping networks on the evolution of trust (barter exchange). The parameters are $x = 0.4$, $b = 0.4$, and $a = 1$. Shares of trust diverge for the dynamic overlaps in both networks.

demonstrates that the frequencies of individuals who trust diverge according to different forms of overlapping networks: some overlapping networks ($p = 0.7$ and $p = 1$) support the evolution of trust, whereas others ($p = 0.3$ and $p = 0$) lead to exploitation. In particular, this changes sharply round the 200th generation and stabilizes around the 300th in all forms of overlapping networks. In this respect, the learning process affects the evolution of trust in the barter process through dynamic overlapping in the interaction network in both a theoretical and a practical sense. For example, since the debt crisis in 2008, many people in Volos in Greece buy and sell through bartering. In order to improve trust, evidence suggests that information sharing helps people know various commodities in the market and identify good or bad traders. This information sharing helps achieve the partly overlapping structure in interactions, thus promoting trust.

Equilibrium frequency of trust

Strategy updating rules are based on probabilistic updating (i.e., the probability of a person altering his or her behavior to that of his or her neighbor is proportional to the payoff received). From a theoretical perspective (e.g., Santos *et al.*, 2006), it is thus necessary to achieve equilibrium frequencies by averaging them over many simulations to draw a general conclusion. As the previous subsection described, experiments are performed on an interaction (scale-free) network with a population of 1,000 and average degree of 2. At the beginning of evolution, equal percentages of individuals followed trust and exploitation strategies in the interaction network. Moreover, this interaction network has remained static throughout evolution, whereas the learning network is generated by the dynamic overlapping model. The equilibrium frequencies of trust strategies derive from a function of the parameters $(a + x)$ and b by averaging over 1,000 generations after a transient time of 10,000 generations (Santos *et al.*, 2006). The final results come from averaging 40 simulations, which means regenerating overlapping models 40 times and averaging their results (see Figure 6.7).

Figure 6.7 shows the equilibrium frequencies of trust in overlapping networks as a function of the parameters $(a + x)$ and b. Being dynamically higher, overlapping networks with $p = 0.7$ support the evolution of trust in the barter economy. Indeed, when both networks coincide, this is problematic for trust, whereas when neither network overlaps, trust erodes. By maintaining the result in non-overlapping networks ($p = 0$) as a benchmark, we observe that in highly dynamic overlapping networks ($p = 0.7$), the equilibrium frequencies of trust rely on the degree of overlapping (having a positive correlation), whereas in wholly dynamic overlapping networks ($p = 1$) there is a sudden change. There results demonstrate that a self-organizing phenomenon from this dynamically overlapping effect exists to enforce the evolution of trust, because the real world is presumably a partly overlapping network that supports trust by some self-organizing phenomenon.

Summary

The results presented in this chapter show that overlapping networks may promote the evolution of trust (see Figures 6.6 and 6.7). Although the theory of stochastic dynamics applied in this chapter partially explains the variety of changes in trust, I account for structured interactions in overlapping networks, since noise is created in the evolutionary process, leading to varieties of change in trust (see Figure 6.6). In particular, together with this discovery, a self-organizing phenomenon was shown that may reduce the negative impact of bartering on the evolution of trust (i.e., destroying trust over time), in contrast to what happens in partly and highly overlapping networks, which enhance trust.

However, some issues remain. For example, evolution was carried out in a finite population similar to that under replicator dynamics (Gintis, 2000; Hauert and Doebeli, 2004; Santos *et al.*, 2006). This issue, which attempts to change the context of the infinite population to the finite population, emphasizes the fact that in the short run the population is finite. In some

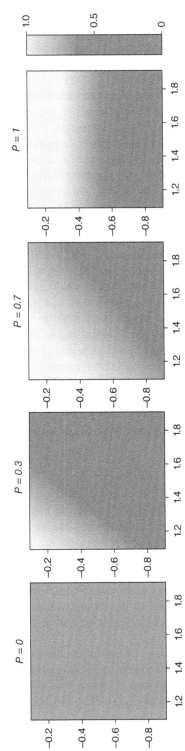

Figure 6.7 Fixing the equilibrium frequencies of trust as a function of the parameters $(a + x)$ and b. $(1 \leq (a + x) \leq 2$ and $-1 \leq b \leq 0)$.

Source: Zhang (2004).

sense, this is intuitive. Nevertheless, as the population is infinite, what would happen in overlapping networks is still unclear and this remains a point for future research. Here, I only considered the evolution of trust in a barter economy, which implies that the same conclusions for Internet and monetary exchanges may be far-fetched. This point might also be an avenue for future studies.

References

Barabási, A., Albert, R. 1999. Emergence of Scaling in Random Networks. *Science*, 286(5439), 509–512.

Emerson, R.M. 1978. Power, Equity and Commitment in Exchange Networks. *American Sociological Review*, 43, 721–739.

Foster, D., Young, P. 1990. Stochastic Evolutionary Game Dynamics. *Theoretical Population Biology*, 38(2), 219–232.

Freidlin, M.I., Wentzell, A.D. 1994. *Random Perturbations of Dynamical Systems*. Berlin: Springer-Verlag.

Gintis, H. 2000. *Game Theory Evolving*. Princeton, NJ: Princeton University Press.

Güth, W., Kliemt, H. 2004. The Evolution of Trust (Worthiness) in the Net. *Analyse & Kritik*, 26, 203–219.

Hardin, R. 2001. Norms of Cooperativeness and Networks of Trust. In: Hechter, M., Opp, K.D. (Eds), *Social Norms*. New York, NY: Russell Sage Foundation, 191–221.

Hardin, R. 2006. *Trust: Key Concepts*. Cambridge, UK: Polity Press.

Hauert, C., Doebeli, M. 2004. Spatial Structure Often Inhibits the Evolution of Cooperation in the Snowdrift Game. *Nature*, 428, 643–646.

Nowak, M.A., Sasaki, A., Taylor, C., Fudenberg, D. 2004. Emergence of Cooperation and Evolutionary Stability in Finite Populations. *Nature*, 428, 646–650.

Santos, F.C., Pacheco, J.M., Lenaerts, T. 2006. Evolutionary Dynamics of Social Dilemmas in Structured Heterogeneous Populations. *PNAS*, 103(9), 3490–3494.

Suzuki, R., Arita, T. 2009. Evolution of Cooperation on Different Pairs of Interaction and Replacement Networks with Various Intensity of Selection. *IEEE Congress on Evolutionary Computation*, 494–499.

Wilensky, U. 2005. *NetLogo Preferential Attachment Model*. Center for Connected Learning and Computer-Based Modeling, Northwestern Institute on Complex Systems, Northwestern University, Evanston, IL. Available at: http://ccl.north western.edu/netlogo/models/PreferentialAttachment (accessed 23 September 2012).

Young, H.P. 1998. *Individual Strategy and Social Structure: An Evolutionary Theory of Institutions*. Princeton, NJ: Princeton University Press.

Zhang, YL. 2014. Partially and Wholly Overlapping Networks: The Evolutionary Dyanmics of Social Dilemmas on Social Networks. *Computational Economics*. Forthcoming. Doi: DOI 10.1007/s10614-014-9447-6.

7 Conclusions

As argued in Chapter 1, the purpose of this study was to focus on the exchange–trust relationship by emphasizing the different effects of barter, monetary, and Internet exchanges on interactive trust phenomena in order to provide a co-evolving theory of exchange systems and trust. This motivation was then specified into four research questions and the framework that guided the analysis in this study. The four research questions were defined as follows:

1 How can trust emerge in exchange?
2 After its emergence, how does exchange affect trust in the dynamic process (i.e., how does trust evolve)?
3 When are the dynamics of trust stable?
4 Do interactive trust phenomena differ under different exchange systems (e.g., barter, monetary, Internet)?

Moreover, the framework was designed in two parts: the theoretical foundation (i.e., the theory of the system of trust) and an analytical approach (i.e., the evolutionary approach).

Chapters 2 and 3 introduced the method and theoretical foundations for a co-evolving theory of exchange systems and trust in which particular interactive structures that arise from exchange systems were formalized. Chapters 4 to 6 dealt with the research questions above in detail. Chapter 4, related to research question 1, provided two contexts (behavioral and evolutionary interdependences) with different trust concepts (expectation, reason, calculation, and imitation) to analyze the emergence of trust. Chapter 5 contained a series of mathematical models to answer research questions 2 and 3. I utilized the evolutionary approach in order to characterize the evolution and stability of trust in exchange systems in the narrowest sense and identified the influence of exchange systems on different trust topics in the broadest sense. Chapter 6 addressed turbulence in the dynamics of trust, which affects the final outcome of dynamics under a distinct combination of factors. This chapter also considered the evolution of trust introduced in Chapter 5 more generally and offered implications for the varieties of trust in real life.

The remainder of this chapter draws conclusions in four parts: the core contributions to the body of knowledge on trust and exchange, methodological implications, practical implications, and future research directions.

Core contributions

This study presented a theory of co-evolving trust and exchange systems based on the theory of a system of trust in which the emergence, evolution, stability, and variety of trust in an interactive process were formalized. It thus contributes to research on trust and exchange by proposing a co-evolutionary theory of interactive trust phenomena.

The theory of co-evolution presented herein argued that trust may have co-evolved historically with exchange systems, thereby explaining that exchange is important for trust. In the past, trust was typically studied just as a premise of exchange; however, this study helps answer the second paradox of trust, namely why exchange is not essential for trust, by describing the orientation of the theory and enriching knowledge of this assumption. In particular, it also explains that different types of exchanges act upon different sides of interactive trust phenomena. This theory addresses the first paradox of trust, namely how people constrain self-interest in order to trust. Since trust is rational and conditional (see Chapter 4), if its requirements are satisfied, it is placed by people, which answers the paradox of trust. To describe the specific contributions of this work, I next elaborate on the findings from the three main research questions (i.e., research questions 1–3).

The core points obtained for the first research question imply a new principle for the emergence of trust, namely that it requires a combination of interdependence forms and structures. This argument is explained in Chapter 4 by considering the interdependent structure of barter exchange with behavioral and evolutionary interdependences. In behavioral interdependence, the emergence of trust is related to a rational choice approach to trust, characterized as people making rational decisions based on expectation, reason, and calculation. These conditions re-emphasize the fact that trust is rational and conditional and that "under appropriate conditions, trust can be recommended to rational persons" (Bruni and Sugden, 2000, p. 23). In evolutionary interdependence, the emergence of trust is placed into an imitating context, in which a theoretical method of imitation is introduced that extends the domain of the study of trust. A model of the emergence of trust in the barter economy, together with a consideration of imitation, was presented to show how trust emerges in this process. Overall, in this chapter a systematic framework and analysis was devoted to answering this research question, thus offering a reference for future studies, especially when considering the relationship between exchange and the emergence of trust.

The core points obtained for the second research question confirm the expectations based on the theoretical foundation presented in Chapter 2 and realistic observations discussed in Chapter 5 (see section "The phenomena of the co-evolution of trust and exchange systems: Trust in barter and monetary economies"), namely that the evolution of trust is affected by exchange and constrained by different exchanges because of their structures. Here, I used the evolutionary approach, particularly replicator dynamic models (see Chapter 3, section "Basic concepts"), to describe the evolution process of trust in different exchange settings. The outcome shows that the evolution of trust in barter exchange generates a decreasing trajectory over time, whereas that in monetary and Internet exchanges is represented by various development trends (see Chapter 5, section "Micro-to-macro transition of trust in exchange systems: Trust in different interactive structures and populations"). These findings confirm that barter exchange does not enhance the evolution of trust, whereas monetary and Internet exchanges do under certain circumstances. These points have been overlooked by studies of exchange and trust so far.

In order to consider the evolution of trust in exchange more generally, noise was introduced into the argument in Chapter 6. Dynamic processes may be influenced by many kinds of noises such as migration factors, spatial structures, and institutions, making it necessary to show the function of noise on the evolution of trust. Under this circumstance, the evolution of trust was placed into overlapping networks (see Chapter 6, section "Trust in overlapping networks: Noise and varieties of change") because a certain noise is created by the structured interactions in interaction and learning processes. In this network model, varieties of change in trust were presented based on the degree of overlap between interaction and learning networks (see Figures 6.6 and 6.7). In particular, the outcome implied the existence of self-organizing phenomena that encourage self-interested people to trust spontaneously, provided two kinds of networks overlap over time (see Figure 6.7). In some sense, this finding contributes to research on the evolution of trust by providing certain noises from overlapping networks and identifying more reason for varieties of changes in trust to exist.

The core points obtained for the third research question show that the stability of trust may come from exchange systems themselves, rather than from trust. To pursue this purpose, two stability analysis methods from the evolutionary approach were applied, namely static and dynamic predictions. In the static prediction, through the concept of ESSs (Weibull, 1995), I showed that trust in barter exchange is an *unstable strategy*, in monetary exchange is a *single weakly stable strategy*, and in Internet exchange is a *double weakly stable strategy* (see Propositions 5.1–5.3). In the dynamic prediction, based on the concept of SSs (Taylor and Jonker, 1978), trust was unable to be verified as an SS in dynamic barter and monetary exchanges, but was shown to be a final SS in dynamic Internet exchange when the condition $m > x$ is satisfied (i.e., enforcement is larger than the profits generated from defection). This allowed for concluding a general theory on the stability of trust in large economies because exchange systems provide distinct points for the stability of trust.

Methodological applications

This study utilized an evolutionary approach to analyze the emergence, evolution, and stability of trust, while game theory was applied to create the theoretical foundation and understand the emergence of trust. Using this approach allowed for contributing to the body of research in terms of the four research questions as well as enhancing previous studies of trust and exchange.

This approach grasps two important points for analysis: (i) the interactive context of exchange and trust is supported, and (ii) there is a theoretical foundation for analyzing interactive trust phenomena (i.e., emergence, evolution, and stability). In particular, it helps show the differences between the exchange systems of interactive trust phenomena. For example, the evolution of trust is unsupported by barter exchange but partly supported by monetary and Internet exchanges in some situations (see Chapter 5, section "Micro-to-macro transition of trust in exchange systems: Trust in different interactive structures and populations"). This finding contrasts with the unification of the trust–exchange relation considered in previous studies, thereby achieving a co-evolving theory of exchange systems and trust. Therefore, these advantages offer a methodological frame for future studies.

The approach applied in this study also extends the domain of studies of trust and exchange. Because it is independent of a rationality-based methodology (e.g., Deutsch, 1973), an institution-based methodology (e.g., Knight, 1990), or an empiricism-based methodology (e.g., Knack and Philip, 1997), which form the basis of the evolutionary perspective, it emphasizes the importance of interdependent forms and structures on interactive phenomena. However, because exchange was considered to be a basic interactive process, together with (interdependent) exchange structures and behavioral and evolutionary interdependences, which affect interactive trust phenomena in a society, various interactive processes and interdependent structures emerged. This finding suggests that the evolutionary approach is sufficient to consider trust or exchange in a series of treatments as long as an interactive context is rearranged. For example, considering public good interactions on trust to analyze its emergence, evolution, and stability would be suitable for this approach.

Implications

The importance of trust was described in Chapter 1 according to TCT (e.g., Williamson, 1985), agency theory (e.g., Ross, 1973), and expectation theory (e.g., Luhmann, 1979). However, a correlation between dynamic exchange and trust and between this dynamic process and interactive trust phenomena (i.e., emergence, evolution, stability) is lacking. Chapter 2 presented a co-evolving theory of exchange systems and trust based on the theory of the system of trust provided by Coleman (1990). This theory suggests that interdependent structures exist in barter, monetary, and Internet exchanges and stresses the importance of the latter on trust phenomena in dynamic exchanges. Chapters 4, 5, and 6 discussed the emergence, evolution, and stability of trust under these structures, respectively. These contributions illustrated that distinct exchange systems lead to different properties of trust phenomena in interactive contexts, as interdependent structures are inherent, offering practical implications.

First, the main components of the present study shed light on improving trust, which is crucial, in two steps. On the one hand, the analysis of the interdependence structures in which trust is embedded is a premise of the generation of trust in interactive contexts. As Chapter 2 outlined, trust enters into different interdependence structures and exchange systems, while distinct interactive trust phenomena are taken for granted (see Chapter 5). These theoretical findings suggest that trust is path-dependent, the improvement of which is largely contingent on interdependent structures. On the other hand, interdependence forms as important points must be considered. In Chapters 4 and 5, this study introduced behavioral and evolutionary interdependences, which showed interactive trust phenomena with interdependence forms and different conditions.

Second, if trust is improved, design may enhance economic growth. Because trust is strongly related to economic growth (Knack and Zak, 2002), exchange – as the main interactive context for connecting people struggling to survive in a society – affects trust from the micro to the macro levels of interaction. Finally, the state of society can lead to trust if certain conditions are satisfied (see Chapters 4 and 5). In this sense, this study extends recent empirical studies of trust and economic growth because it offers an interactive process and explains why trust emerges, evolves, and stabilizes. It also suggests that an economic growth model may focus on the interdependent structures in which trust is embedded in exchange because different structures lead to different trust phenomena (see Chapter 5). Therefore, institutions should exogenously or endogenously influence micro-interdependent structures to improve trust in society and further enhance economic growth.

In addition, this study serves as a framework for the mechanism design of trust in exchange systems because it analyzed and drew conclusions on how exchange systems affect trust, resulting in co-evolving phenomena. No matter what kind of exchange system emerges, the theoretical treatment of barter, monetary, and Internet systems in this study is devoted to improving the levels of trust inherent in them.

Future research directions

Despite the contributions to the research topic listed in section "Methodological applications" above, several knowledge gaps remain. For example, in Chapter 4, the emergence of trust with imitation dynamics was only considered in barter exchange, not in monetary and Internet exchanges. In Chapter 5, the relationship between barter shares and trust was implicitly presented because data are limited. Meanwhile, the meso level of evolution (Elsner and Schwardt, 2014) was not considered in this chapter. In Chapter 6, trust in overlapping networks was also only placed in barter exchange. Overall, these gaps may suggest research avenues for future studies of exchange and trust.

References

Bruni, L., Sugden, R. 2000. Moral Canals: Trust and Social Capital in the Work of Humer, Smith and Genovesi. *Economics and Philosophy*, 16(1), 21–45.

Coleman, J.S. 1990. *Foundations of Social Theory*. Cambridge, MA: Harvard University Press.

Deutsch, M. 1973. *The Resolution of Conflict*. New Haven, CT: Yale University Press.

Elsner, W., Schwardt, H. 2014. Trust and Arena Size: Expectations, Institutions, and General Trust, and Critical Population and Group Sizes. *Journal of Institutional Economics*, 10(1), 107–134.

Knack, S., Philip, K. 1997. Does Social Capital have a Payoff? A Cross-Country Investigation. *Quarterly Journal of Economics*, 112(4), 1251–1288.

Knack, S., Zak, P.J. 2002. Building Trust: Public Policy, Interpersonal Trust, and Economic Development. *Supreme Court Economic Review*, 10, 91–107.

Knight, J. 1990. *Institutions and Social Conflict*. Cambridge, MA: Cambridge University Press.

Luhmann, N. 1979. *Trust and Power: Two Works by Niklas Luhmann*. Translation of German Originals, Vertrauen (1968) and Macht (1975). Chichester: John Wiley.

Ross, S. 1973. The Economic Theory of Agency: The Principle's Problem. *American Economic Review*, 63(2), 134–139.

Taylor, P., Jonker, L. 1978. Evolutionary Stable Strategies and Game Dynamics. *Mathematical Biosciences*, 40, 145–156.

Weibull, J.W. 1995. *Evolutionary Game Theory*. London: MIT Press.

Williamson, O.E. 1985. *The Economic Institutions of Capitalism*: *Firms, Markets, Relational Contracting*. New York, NY: Free Press.

Index

For Product Safety Concerns and Information please contact our EU
representative GPSR@taylorandfrancis.com Taylor & Francis Verlag GmbH,
Kaufingerstraße 24, 80331 München, Germany

Printed and bound by CPI Group (UK) Ltd, Croydon, CR0 4YY
01/05/2025
01858438-0001